WHAT IF I SAY THE WRONG THING?

WHAT IF I SAY THE WR⚬NG THING?

25 HABITS FOR CULTURALLY EFFECTIVE PEOPLE

VERNĀ A. MYERS

AMERICAN**BAR**ASSOCIATION

ABA Publishing

Cover design by Elmarie Jara / ABA Publishing.

The materials contained herein represent the opinions of the authors and/or the editors, and should not be construed to be the views or opinions of the law firms or companies with whom such persons are in partnership with, associated with, or employed by, nor of the American Bar Association or the ABA Section of International Law and the ABA Diversity Center unless adopted pursuant to the bylaws of the Association.

Nothing contained in this book is to be considered as the rendering of legal advice for specific cases, and readers are responsible for obtaining such advice from their own legal counsel. This book is intended for educational and informational purposes only.

Printed in the United States of America.

24 23   22 21 20

Library of Congress Cataloging-in-Publication Data

Myers, Verna.
  What if I say the wrong thing? : 25 habits for culturally effective people / Verna Myers, American Bar Association.
    pages cm
  This book is a follow-up to Moving diversity forward, 2011.
  Includes bibliographical references and index.
  ISBN 978-1-61438-971-2
  1. Law firms--United States--Personnel management. 2. Diversity in the workplace--United States. 3. Political correctness--United States. I. Myers, Verna. Moving diversity forward. II. Title.
  KF300.M944 2013
  340.068'3--dc23
                    2013025576

Discounts are available for books ordered in bulk. Special consideration is given to state bars, CLE programs, and other bar related organizations. Inquire at Book Publishing, ABA Publishing, American Bar Association, 321 N. Clark Street, Chicago, Illinois 60654-7598.

www.ShopABA.org

To my nieces and nephews, whose dreams strengthen my resolve

CONTENTS

ABOUT THE AUTHOR

Vernā Myers, Esq., principal of Vernā Myers Consulting Group, LLC (VMCG), is an internationally recognized expert on diversity and inclusion, specializing in the legal field. Vernā is a dynamic speaker and creative advisor in support of creating inclusive environments and improving the recruitment and retention of underrepresented groups. Ms. Myers is well known for her expansive approach to diversity and her belief that inclusion is necessary for people from different cultures, ethnicities, genders, generations, physical abilities, races, sexual orientations, experiences, and backgrounds to thrive in their organizations. When these individuals excel, organizations realize the power of diversity.

VMCG has collaborated with over 100 clients to effect sustainable organizational change by conducting cultural assessments, developing comprehensive strategic diversity action plans informed by her knowledge of cross-cultural competencies, and facilitating compelling and interactive workshops in the United States and around the globe. A highly sought-after speaker at numerous conferences worldwide, Vernā sponsors the highly successful annual Opus Conference on Race and Ethnicity in Large Law Firms, and frequently is the keynote speaker at bar and legal association meetings, leadership retreats, women's conferences, and affinity group forums. Vernā has worked internationally for a number of global law firms with offices in the United Kingdom, Germany, China, Japan, Singapore, Canada, Sweden, and Russia.

Vernā is the author of *Moving Diversity Forward: How to Go from Well-Meaning to Well-Doing*, published by the American Bar Association in 2011. http://www.movingdiversityforward.com.

In 2010, Pepper Hamilton LLP awarded Ms. Myers its Diversity Champion award. In 2009 she was chosen as one of *The Network Journal*'s "25 Influential Black Women in Business," and in 2008, one of *The Massachusetts Lawyers Weekly*'s "Diversity Heroes."

Prior to establishing VMCG, Vernā was the first Executive Director of the Boston Law Firm Group, a consortium of firms committed to increasing racial/ethnic diversity. She served as Deputy Chief of Staff for the Attorney General of Massachusetts (1997–99), where she executed a comprehensive diversity and inclusion initiative: increasing minority recruitment, conducting diversity and sexual harassment trainings, and performing outreach to the state's diverse population. Vernā practiced corporate and real estate law in Boston for six years at Testa, Hurwitz & Thibeault, LLP and Fitch, Wiley, Richlin & Tourse, LLP.

Vernā graduated from Harvard Law School and received a Bachelor of Arts, *magna cum laude*, from Barnard College, Columbia University. She resides in her hometown of Baltimore, Maryland.

Follow Vernā on Twitter @vernamyers or visit her at http://www.vernamyers consulting.com and movingdiversityforward.com.

ACKNOWLEDGMENTS

Thanks to everyone who has shared with me their stories of triumph and trouble, anxiety, anger, and apology as they travel this worthwhile but sometimes challenging diversity journey. I have taken those stories and my own stumbles to create a book that hopefully offers Habits to smooth out some of the rough patches and keep us moving diversity forward. I would like to acknowledge the great team who helped to make this book possible. I want to thank my wonderful editor, Stuart Horwitz of Book Architecture, for his valuable advice and editing even as he was in the demanding process of having his own book published and released! Congratulations! I also must give my good friend and fellow author, Susanne Goldstein, credit for giving me the idea of a tip book and helping to refine its title and organization. I really appreciate Tim Brandhorst and his team at ABA Publishing for their enthusiastic welcome and support.

Thanks to Amy Allbright and Rye Young for sharing information to improve specific tips for interacting effectively with those in the disability and transgender communities. Thanks to Valerie Batts of Visions, Inc., who first introduced me to a version of the chart on page 3, my unearned one-up groups, and the truth of internalized oppression. I am grateful to Scott Harshbarger for propelling my confidence and career and his willingness to let me use him in the last Habit as an example of what it means to be a true sponsor.

I want to thank my VMCG team. Without their professionalism and dedication, I would not be able to run around the country consulting and also write books. Thanks to the incomparable Jennifer Simpson, who cares deeply about the work of VMCG and getting me to the right place at the right time. It's not an easy job. I appreciate the wisdom of Jane Bermont, our Director of Client Services, that helps me make change by using my gifts in a strategic way. Thanks to Catherine Moore, our great researcher, and all the VMCG consultants who work diligently and hopefully with our clients to create sustainable change. My deepest gratitude also goes to my friend, Sheila Hubbard, for being the one who agrees with me to constantly commit all my endeavors, including this one, to prayer.

This book is not about perfection; it is about overcoming the fear of connection. So I want to thank my family—my mom and dad, sister and brother, nieces and nephews, uncles and aunts, and, of course, my precious son for teaching me that perfect love casts out all fear.

INTRODUCTION

A couple of years ago, I wrote a book called *Moving Diversity Forward: How to Go from Well-Meaning to Well-Doing*, because so many of my well-meaning friends and clients wanted to put their feet where their hearts were. They wanted to know what they could do to see more diversity in their workplaces and communities and how they could build authentic relationships across race. In *Moving Diversity Forward*, I discussed in depth the fundamental concepts of diversity and inclusion, examined the barriers to diversity progress, and offered steps that individuals and organizations could take to make a difference.

I created this new "tip book" as way to keep your diversity journey moving. I wanted to remind you of things we learned in the first book by making the information quick, bite-sized, and accessible. So many people come up to me after a workshop or speech and ask me the "What should I do?" questions: "What if I say the wrong thing, what should I do?" "What if I am at work and someone makes a sexist joke, what should I say?" They are looking to develop the habits of culturally effective people. They are committed to moving diversity forward.

This book is designed to answer some of these questions about various types of diversity issues and start you practicing culturally effective habits. My hope is that by seeing a number of different situations, with a variety of suggested follow-ups and actions, you will better know how to handle your own situation. Many of these scenarios occur without us being "properly prepared" for them; reading these habits is like doing drills so you'll be ready!

You can turn to these tips whenever you need them. Use this new book at your discretion, or when you feel like you would like a little infusion of inspiration. And you can always go back to the first book if you want a deeper dive on a certain subject.

You might also want to give this book or just one of the chapters to a friend or colleague who you know could use it, either because she's experiencing one of the stories in this book or because he might avoid one of the situations, if only he or she knew the culturally effective way to approach it.

So, here we go together—preparing, practicing, and moving diversity forward!

Vernā A. Myers
Baltimore
August, 2013

WHAT IF I SAY THE WRONG THING?

25 HABITS FOR CULTURALLY EFFECTIVE PEOPLE

HABIT #1: BUT I'M NOT A RACIST!
UNDERSTAND THE *ISMS*

I had the opportunity to interview the top leader of a large century-old public service organization. The organization was 87 percent white and the racial minorities in the organization were seriously upset about their persistent and severe underrepresentation and the racial mistreatment they perceived. VMCG, my consulting firm, had been asked to assist. During the interview, the earnest and open-minded leader of this well-respected institution said, "I have been here for 25 years, and I have never seen one act of racism...and I believe everyone here is like me. We would never intentionally discriminate against anyone. In fact, I'm offended that I am being accused of being a racist."

His comments echoed those of the many leaders I encounter in corporations who scratch their heads over the scarcity of women among their highest ranks. They tell me, "We want to see women succeed here, we know women are among the smartest and talented people we have—this is not a sexist institution." When I mentioned the concept of "group oppression" to one leader, he told me, "You can't use that word here. People make too much money here to be oppressed. No one is putting arm bands on people; if they don't like it here, they can always leave."

Repeatedly, in these situations, I want to show them the chart below. I want to walk these sincere and sometimes personally wounded individuals through the dynamic of the *isms* (racism, sexism, elitism, etc.) and the reality of a structure that is invisible to them but operates to maintain the status quo in their organizations and our society. Sometimes I can, but, for many, this culturally effective step of seeing the problem as structural rather than personal seems too threatening and enormous. You have picked up this book, so I am assuming you want to delve into the chart on the next page and understand how group oppression works.

Culturally Ineffective: "I'm not racist; I'm a good person"

We start the conversation on moving diversity forward with two fundamental aware-nesses. The first is that even if you are a "good person," all people, including "good people," have been influenced and shaped not only by racism, but by all of the *isms* on the chart. The second awareness is that even if you could avoid participating, the *isms* would still exist. Systemic oppression of various groups does not need your intentional or unintentional involvement in order to be alive and operational in our institutions. It is already embedded therein and is self-perpetuating. And it will continue until "good people" become the culturally effective people and even then will take big changes to dismantle.

As you take time to look at the chart, you can find yourself in either a "one-up" or "one-down" group depending on each category. One-up means the particular group has been identified by our American society in a way that gives the people in that group a leg up from the beginning whether they want it or not. I have chosen to use "one-up" and "one-down" rather than terms like "dominant vs. subordinate" or "superior vs. inferior" because to my mind, one-up vs. one-down is a construct less laden with destructive energy. You may remember this chart from *Moving Diversity Forward*. I used the terms "Historically Advantaged (Nontarget Group)" and "(Historically Dis-advantaged (Target Group)." I have chosen to use "one-up" and "one-down" rather than Historically Advantaged and Disadvantaged because throughout this book you will see how these designations, although antiquated and erroneous, continue to have an impact on our lives. Sometimes I will talk about more privilege or less privilege to refer to these groups. The intent is not to dwell on the terms, of course, or be triggered

Historically Advantaged and Disadvantaged
A Group Analysis for the United States

Type of Oppression "Ism"	Variable	One-up	One-down
Racism	Race/ethnicity/ color	White	People of color: (African, Asian, Native, Latino/a)
Sexism	Gender	Men	Women, transgendered
Homophobia/ heterosexism	Sexual Orientation	Heterosexuals	LGBT individuals
Religious oppression/ anti-Semitism/ Islamophobia	Religion	Protestants	Catholics, Jews, Muslims, Sikhs
Classism	Socioeconomic Class	Owning, upper and middle class, managerial	Poor, working class, wage workers
Elitism	Education level/ place in hierarchy	College–educated; top 20–40 schools	Not college-educated; less prestigious schools
Xenophobia	Immigrant status	U.S. born	Immigrants
Linguistic oppression	Language	English speakers	Non–English speakers
Ableism	Physical or mental ability	Able-bodied persons (body/mind)	People with disabilities
Ageism/adultism	Age	Adults	Elders: 40+ by law; children, youth
Militarism	Military status	WWI, WWII, Korean Veterans	Vietnam, Gulf War (I & II) veterans

(Adapted from Visions, Inc.)

3

into a defensive reaction by them, but to understand that there is a framework for the discussion of diversity, inclusion, and cultural effectiveness.

Often, in the news, when there is yet another racial incident, people interviewed who believe they know the accused will say, "I don't think this was racism" or "I know her well and she's not a racist; she grew up in an integrated neighborhood (or is a victim of an older generation)." Every time I hear comments like this, I think, "Really? How did she do that—escape racism, that is?" To be culturally effective when it comes to the *isms* we have to be willing to accept that we were all outside when the fallout happened and that in lots of ways we all caught the message that our one-up groups are intellectually, culturally, and morally superior to all other one-down groups. This message was showered upon all of us and it penetrated the soil of our culture. This has happened to everyone without escape. Even the people who had great parents who taught them to treat everyone with respect and fairness? Yes. What about the people who never noticed these distinctions? Yes. Even people from the one-down groups themselves? Yep. And if we accept that we have been shaped by these beliefs, we have to accept that when good people are on the one-up side, sometimes they act in ways that are guided by and responsive to a particular *ism*.

If we want to reserve the term "racist" or "sexist" (or any other "-ists") for those who consciously and explicitly hold and intentionally act on beliefs of superiority, then many of us are safe! Most of us are not "racist." However, investing our sense of self in this definition of "racist" may not get us very far if we hope to be culturally effective and inclusive in our relationships and organizations. You will learn, as you read further in this book, that not all our biases are conscious or intentional, so even when we don't want to behave in accordance with the antiquated and misguided beliefs about one group of people being inferior to another, we nevertheless sometimes do.

4

In other words, whether something is racism or sexism, it is not only about our interpersonal behavior, intentional or unconscious, toward individuals. We are operating within and trying to contend with a system of power and privilege that advantages some groups over others because of old-fashioned ideas of superiority and inferiority. This self-sustaining system of inequality is called structural or systemic racism (sexism, etc.). Structural *isms* result because the institution or practice was created by and for the one-up group only—other groups, seen as inferior, were excluded or ignored at the inception of the policy, practice, or organization.

Let's take a concrete example of structural exclusion. Those who were responsible for planning and erecting our buildings, transit systems, and city blocks years ago were without physical disabilities. Therefore they built structures that made sense for people who were like they were, but by doing so, they created unintentional barriers that disadvantaged people who had disabilities. No matter how skilled a person with an ambulatory disability is at maneuvering themselves, without curb cuts and ramps, he or she is disadvantaged as compared to those of us who can walk.

This example seems too obvious for anyone to deny. We believe a person with disabilities when they tell us about the difficulties they experience using a non-equipped facility. We need to make the move to believing what people from all one-down groups say about their experiences of exclusion and bias. Assume that it is hard for you to know in your one-up status how the subtle bias and the structural difficulties affect a particular one-down group.

We need to recognize that in many ways we are like a fish that doesn't see the water. Our environments were built for us. The white male leaders of the companies I described above, who wonder why there are not more people of color or women, often look to see if there are individuals in their organizations—bad apples—who are acting out of personal animus against a group. When they don't see blatant acts of bigotry, they are stumped. They don't realize that individuals in a one-down group sometimes fail to reach their potential or feel excluded, unseen, and disrespected because the institution was not built for them; the recipe for failure was already baked into the cake when they arrived. Even if these individuals don't mind being severely underrepresented in the organization, and they work hard and take a great deal of personal responsibility for their success, policies that appear neutral on their face actually construct impediments that those in the one-up group do not have to manage. A culturally effective person accounts for the existence of not only personal bias (conscious and unconscious) but also institutional barriers. In fact, to be culturally effective in supporting one-down groups, being a "good person" is not enough. You have to do something about the system, like creating curb cuts, erecting ramps and widening entrances; being passive can yield the same results as being bigoted.

Tips for Practicing This Culturally Effective Habit: Understand the *Isms*

- Get out of the need to deny the *isms* or make a declaration about how "good a person" you are or how you love everyone. When people from a one-down group hear these things, they have a hard time seeing you as an ally. Start saying things like, "Well, as a straight person, I am sure I have some misinformation about gay people, but I am willing to unlearn it." Or, "I grew up having more than enough, so sometimes I make assumptions about people who had less—I am sure I have no idea what it was like for you."
- Learn more about the disparities in employment, justice, housing, education, and health care, critical factors that affect life chances for success. Ask yourself questions like, Why are black and brown people overrepresented in our prisons? Why are there not more people with visible disabilities in the legal profession? Don't stop at the surface explanations either.

- Look for the systems and connect the dots. In other words, don't just examine the interpersonal behaviors and relationships you see around your institution, department, neighborhood, club, or school, but the systemic barriers in policies, practices, and operations that might make it harder for one-down group members to excel or feel respected in the environment. For example, is it required that anyone who wants to get promoted to the Vice President of Sales in your company, move around every two years to different offices of the company? This is an example of a neutral system—a requirement for everyone for which there is a rationale. But when you ask why more women aren't VPs, consider the degree of difficulty women face trying to satisfy this seemingly neutral requirement as compared to men. Few people (man or woman) want to pick up and move every two years. But men, as a group, because of their position on the chart in the gender category, are often differently situated in family power dynamics and responsibility in a way that allows more men to satisfy this obligation than most women. So in actuality it is not a neutral requirement; it favors one group over another.

- Practice explaining the difference between the *isms* and bias or prejudice. Any group in either column of the chart can be biased for or against another group. Pre-judging is not something reserved for the one-up group. But, biases are not the same as *isms*. The *isms* speak to how certain groups have the power and the privilege to act on their biases and prejudices, and to define what is right and good and beautiful and true. It is also about the ability to use that power to maintain dominance and exclude others who are not in that group. I love movies. But when I watch the Academy Awards and most of the actresses and actors are white, and most of the directors and producers are men, I know it's not because these are the best actors, directors and movie ideas out there.

7

There are talented actors of color, female directors, and powerful films about diverse communities, but the barriers built into the motion picture industry, a system originally created by and for white men, make it hard for them to get a footing or the stage to show these talents and stories. Therefore, the white male group, deeply entrenched in the system after years of exclusion of others, has the easier time making and solidifying key relationships, green-lighting projects, and deciding what audiences want to see. If there is a non-diverse group of people making these decisions, it is no surprise that we don't have more films that appeal to, reflect, and utilize diverse talent.

- Support the types of programs, policies, and interventions that organizations are implementing to make up for the disparities and structural impediments to one-down groups, such as scholarships, outreach, mentoring, affinity groups, flexibility, and more time for advancement or examinations. Be the one who explains to those who complain about these programs being unfair and in violation of the principles of merit, why they are needed, and how they help to level the playing field so that actual merit rather than favoritism determines opportunity and advancement.

- Remember the chart above represents a group analysis about larger overarching systems, not about individuals. Individuals can have different outcomes because we have memberships in different groups. Subcultures exist within the bigger U.S. society that can change the dynamic of who is one-up or one-down, but only in that smaller context. For example, in some industries, cities, and communities a one-down group can become large enough that they can overcome exclusion by carving out their own culture. Sometimes even they become oppressive of other groups. This starts out as more of a matter of survival. However, it can move to a sense of superiority over others.

- Make the systems of disadvantage and advantage visible to your children and younger people who may only see the surface and begin to misinterpret the disparities as an indication that some groups of people are less than others. Explain to them that *isms* still exist. Share the history of exclusion, the amazing accomplishments of members from the one-down groups despite the odds, and the important justice work of many from one-up groups. Most importantly, let them know that they need to be part of moving diversity forward by rejecting the old false beliefs in our society and creating more fairness and inclusion.

9

HABIT #2: I HOPE SHE CAN DRIVE
GET FAMILIAR WITH YOUR BIASES

As a seasoned flyer, I was pleasantly shocked one day just as the plane soared to 30,000 feet. The pilot began to speak over the public-address system, and it was the voice of a woman. It's a female pilot! Pilots are so rarely women, and I was thrilled to be riding with a woman who had broken through the glass ceiling but was reigning in the stratosphere. However, later into the flight, we encountered terrible turbulence, and the ride got bumpy. The plane started bouncing up and down, and I thought, *Oh, goodness, I hope she can drive!*

Culturally Ineffective: "I'm So Cool; I've Worked through All of My Biases by Now"

So, I didn't say the wrong thing out loud, but I was thinking it! Not until I was on the return flight with a male pilot and the plane began to experience turbulence did I notice my gender bias. Before that I had been so worried that it didn't even occur to me that my thinking was the problem. Where did my bias come from? After all, I am a woman and I can drive and I know many men who can't.

When I thought about it more deeply, I realized that the pilot is almost always a man and it is often a bumpy ride. I couldn't ever remember thinking about a male pilot, *I hope he knows how to work this vehicle.* Yes, I have been afraid for my ultimate safety. And I've wished I had read the safety card in the seat pocket in front of me and watched the video more carefully, but I have never questioned the competence of the pilot through the lens of gender. I have never wondered if he was qualified. At the beginning of the trip, when I heard there was a woman at the helm, I was cheering for diversity! But the minute there was a problem, I lost my enthusiasm.

WHAT IF I SAY THE WRONG THING: 25 HABITS FOR CULTURALLY EFFECTIVE PEOPLE

We all have biases. Some of them are implicit—meaning they are unconscious and we are largely unaware of them—while some are explicit and conscious. Biases can often be particularly strong in stressful situations, which are unfortunately one of the worst times to deal with them. It is far better to have assessed our internal landscape prior to hard times.

Getting familiar with your biases is the first step in moving diversity forward. It comes before stopping a particular train of thought or taking positive steps such as getting more information, stepping forward, and making changes. Actually, the first step may be acknowledging that you actually *do* have biases. This can, in fact, be a real problem for well-meaning people who hate to believe they have biases; it goes against their image of themselves.

But this effort is about moving from well-meaning to "well-doing." When your biases present themselves, don't push them away. And please don't say what I have heard some people claim: "I know this is biased, but I can't help how I feel" or "Well, if it's unconscious, what can I do about it?" Our biases came from somewhere—from years of living in a society that has struggled to rid itself of the designations that some groups are seen as better than others. To become capable of being well-doing, we must first become familiar with our biases and use our explicit good beliefs to work hard to counter them. If we don't, the social scientists tell us that our implicit thoughts, not our explicit ones, will be the most accurate predictors of our actual behavior.

Tips for Practicing This Culturally Effective Habit: Get Familiar with Your Biases

- Realize that having biases isn't about being a good or a bad person—it's about being human. In addition, many biases are unconscious and implicit, rather than conscious and explicit, so you might have to work extra hard to uncover them.

- Notice when and where your biases pop up. Biases are often triggered by stressful situations or instances in which you are not in control. You can actually use these opportunities to become familiar with your implicit biases.
- Don't be surprised if you have biases against your own group. As I mentioned, we are all breathing in the smog of the *isms* and they get reinforced in the most subtle ways every day. Even when we have personal experience and information to negate them, the beliefs behind the *isms* are hard to remove from our thoughts and actions.
- Remind yourself of what you really believe and value—pay attention to what is true instead of what you fear based on your stereotypes and biases. After you make a new (and possibly unwanted) discovery about yourself, you will always have the opportunity to substitute new behaviors that are fair, and act to minimize your bias.
- It might also help to review some of the recent decisions you have made: Whom have you hired? Whom did you sell your house to? Whom did you choose to sit beside on the train? How did you react to your child's new friend? How did you choose your doctor when you joined your new medical insurance carrier? Did these individuals conform to any biases you might be carrying? Did you have a moment where you became aware that they contradicted your biases? When you were reviewing that resume and you saw information possibly indicating the candidate's political affiliation, what thoughts came next? At that moment, did you move towards inclusion or exclusion? Did you work hard to focus on job-related criteria, or did you form an opinion about the candidate's job fit through the lens of your political affiliation? What do you want to do differently the next time?

13

- Test yourself by taking the Implicit Association Test (IAT), developed by scientists to measure biases in several different categories. Each test only takes about ten minutes. The IAT can be sobering but illuminating. http://www.implicit.harvard.edu.

HABIT #3: I'M "FARM"
BE AWARE OF YOUR OWN CULTURE
AND HOW IT SHAPES YOUR INTERACTIONS

In our workshops, we ask participants to look closely at classifications of social identity and life experience and tell us what primary and secondary identities and experiences are the most important to them and why. They look at such subjects as age, race, ethnicity, family status, sexual orientation, sex and gender identity, communication style, hobbies, job responsibility, and physical abilities and qualities. Such an exercise reinforces that we are all diverse; no one person is only one identity. It also helps us become familiar with our "cultural leanings"—how belonging to a certain group or experience influences the very way we see the world. In one session, a man quickly raised his hand and said enthusiastically, "I'm farm." At first I was silent because I thought I hadn't heard him correctly; then I repeated, "You're farm?" "Yes," he said as a few folks chuckled. "Can you explain?" I asked. "Sure. I spent my whole life on a farm, and everything I do has been influenced by that. I can see it all the time in the way I do things and act and expect others to do things. It doesn't always go over so well at work." There was no need to say anything more after he spoke, except "Class dismissed."

Culturally Ineffective: Assuming We Have No Culture or That Our Cultural Background Hasn't Shaped Our Interactions and Worldviews

Each of us looks at the world through our cultural lens. Our unique lens goes beyond being one-up in certain categories or one-down in others; rather, it is an overall blueprint for who we are that is as individual as a snowflake. Cultural awareness is not only about being Latino or gay. Our race, ethnicity, sexual orientation, political views, birth order, marital status, and employment history all contribute to our experience of the world and can be mined when we are unearthing our understanding of values, norms, and how the world is or should be.

Sometimes, during the cultural exploration conversation in our workshops, white, U.S.-born participants will lament that they have no culture. They say, "I am just plain, like white bread." They admire other cultures and wish they had one of their own. Some talk about having lost their culture as prior generations muted or forbade the expression of their culture in order to assimilate successfully. I recognize this truth about assimilation, but I also share good news with them. We all have a culture!! Just as Mr. "I'm Farm" found his, we were all raised with a set of cultural norms, behaviors, values, language, and ways of acting. Sometimes worldviews come from what neighborhood, country, and region of the country we grew up in; whether we lived in a home or apartment, rented or owned; whether we have military experience or spent time in another country as a child. Each of these dimensions of experience creates another aspect of our identity, and all of them can be very important in shaping and filtering our world. Is growing up on a farm a critical factor in shaping your cultural worldview? Absolutely!

Remember also there is a rich dynamic happening between and among cultures and identities, both visible and invisible. For instance, most people would agree that men and women often were taught different ways about how to be in the world, but they assume that all women have the same cultural programming and therefore see the world the same. Yet, things become much more complex when the fact of being a woman is refracted through a woman's racial or ethnic identity, political affiliation, job status, socioeconomic status, hobbies, or religion. Therefore, you can never predict how any individual will see and be in the world based on one identity, experience, or culture—multiple identities, including personality differences make this impossible.

Exploring your own cultural influences is an important prerequisite for moving diversity forward, operating more inclusively, and working against biases and the behaviors that follow from them. For example, you might have been raised to confront authority; your worldview and therefore your bias maybe that those who don't do so lack confidence or lack courage. This means you might completely misunderstand or dismiss a perfectly brave and confident person or group of people. You might believe that the most effective way to respond to conflict is to be direct with your communication and control your emotions because that was what you were taught explicitly or what you observed in your family or community. But in other cultures the way to address conflict is by being indirect and emotionally expressive. If you don't understand that our natural preference for how to resolve conflict is based on culture, you might mistake another person's approach as being ineffective, or worse, irresponsible. These are examples of the different cultural lenses that we all have and through which we view and (mis)interpret the behavior of others. When we lack this awareness, we often end up saying or doing the wrong thing.

This Habit invites you to appreciate the impact of your culture and recognize that your life's experiences and your identities produce certain filters that condition how you see the world. Two decades ago if we were going to undergo cultural training, we would focus on learning the customs, languages, expressions, and values of the other cultures with which we would be doing business. After a while, people realized that this focus addressed only half the picture; at least as important was the recognition that we ourselves are cultural beings with cultural programming that shapes our responses and interpretations. Remember, whenever you are in a

17

culturally uncomfortable situation, you are just as much a factor in the equation as the other person or persons—*and* you're the only one you have any control over!

Tips for Practicing This Culturally Effective Habit: Be Aware of Your Own Culture and How It Shapes Your Interactions

- Spend some time focusing on your own culture and life experiences. Don't only look at the obvious categorizations of gender, sexual orientation, age, race ethnicity, dis(abilities), and so on. Think about the geography of your background, your relationships in childhood, your hobbies, and events that shaped your region and generation. When you were growing up, what did you learn about values, conflict, faith and belief, about work, family obligations, and responsibility? What were you taught about how to dress and talk? From whom did these lessons come? What was forbidden? What was encouraged? Did you grow up in a diverse environment? Who was present? Who was absent?

- The next step is to consider how you live now. How many of these lessons do you still hold on to? Have you rejected some of these teachings? Why? Where have you made shifts in your understanding of the world and how did that happen?

- To be culturally effective in what you say and how you behave toward others, the next important step is to consider how your cultural programming impacts your interactions. How do you see yourself? How do others see you? With whom do you feel comfortable working, living, socializing, partnering, and worshipping? Does your cultural programming make it easier or more challenging for you to embrace people of different backgrounds? Most people find that there are some aspects of their culture that make them afraid, suspicious, or ill-equipped, while other aspects of their backgrounds offer strengths in this area. These questions are keys to finding out more about who you are, what and whom you value, how you interpret the behaviors of others, and why sometimes you say or do the "wrong" thing.

HABIT #4: CAN'T WE ALL JUST GET ALONG?
SEE THE COMMONALITIES BETWEEN PEOPLE

My white friend, Josh, recently went to the funeral of the mother of his close childhood friend. He had just read my book, *Moving Diversity Forward*, about how to be more inclusive of others. At the service, he noticed that everyone at the funeral was white except for one, lone black woman who was not interacting with the rest of the mourners—yet, she herself seemed very distraught over the loss of the deceased. Josh related his thought process this way: "Vernā would say that I should go over and connect with this woman in some way. I feel like I don't know how to approach her or what to say, but just trying will be enough. So, here we go!" A little nervous and awkward, Josh went over and struck up a conversation with the woman, emboldened by the fact that they had at least one thing in common—love and respect for the woman they had lost. During the course of their conversation, Josh discovered that the woman, Judith, had been the longtime nurse who took care of his friend's mother until her death. As Josh spoke with her, she shared with him stories about the woman she had cared for, as well the woman's last words. Josh later told me how blessed he felt by the interaction. By connecting with this person, who was the least like him in the room, he had received the most meaningful pieces of information, which he later shared with his group of friends in a way that eased their suffering. And it had all begun with the assumption that his and Judith's commonalities were greater than their differences.

Culturally Ineffective: "Those People Are Just Too Different from Me"
People we love or trust may have taught us that "those" people are very different from "us" in subtle or not so subtle ways. Overly focusing on difference is one of the

chief reasons we don't see the commonalities among our fellow humans.

Josh was white and male and attending the funeral as a family friend; Judith was black, a woman, and present because she worked for the family. Josh may have picked up on other differences that set Judith apart, such as what she wore or the manner in which she carried herself. The differences, which we misperceive as all-important, can be based on literally anything: some identifying physical feature, race or ethnicity, style, sexual orientation, perceived level of education or socioeconomic class, gender, age, or physical disability. I believe the *isms* are kept in place by the misperceptions about these categories.

I call these the tip-of-the-iceberg identities because human beings are so much more than what you can see. We are all a complex set of identities, cultures, and experiences. Like an iceberg, most of who we are is below the surface. That's the exciting work of cultural effectiveness. You gain the skills to go beyond differences to connect to what you share with individuals. There are a million points of contact when you think of people as multidimensional rather than simply boxing them in by virtue of one identity or attribute. Seeing the commonalities begins when we realize that as human beings we share a basic set of desires. Most of us desire to be loved and happy; to be well and free from suffering; to have food, shelter, and clothing; to enjoy the fruits of our labors; to be engaged in meaningful work; to experience genuine relationships; and to be respected and treated fairly. And not only do we want these things for ourselves, we also want them for our loved ones: our family, our friends, and our close associates.

Learning multicultural skills is the responsibility of all of us, of course. Judith, the nurse at the funeral, was probably very aware of what made her different (race, assumptions about what others did for a living) and may have assumed that she had very little in common with those around her. Someone always needs to reach out first, and

22

it is often easier for the individual in the obvious majority to take the lead. What Josh did, as a white person in a room full of mostly white people, was not only to notice difference, but at the same time to assume commonality. As a result he was enriched and Judith experienced the comfort of recognition and respect, which all of us desire.

Contemplating the things we have in common can lead to a sense of closeness with individuals we may not know as well as those who reside in our inner circle. We are also more likely to see the differences they bring to a certain situation as a positive and not feel removed from or even threatened by them.

One key commonality we share as human beings is that we all know (if we take the time to comb through our life experiences) something about what it feels like to be an outsider or the one who is not valued or is underrepresented. When we are in the one-down position, we know what we would like others to say and do to affirm our humanity and to bring us into the fold. Use the tips to remind yourself to explore, discover, and celebrate the commonalities we share so that you will be motivated like Josh was to cross the floor and close the gaps that create exclusion.

Tips for Practicing This Culturally Effective Habit: See the Commonalities between People

- Always remember that no matter how different from another person you think you are, as human beings you both share significant needs, hopes, desires, and fears. Sometimes these commonalities are expressed and satisfied differently based on different worldviews, but the essence of humanity remains fundamentally the same. This is especially important to keep in mind when you are in a conflict: keeping your adversary human is the ticket to respectful problem solving, while making the other person out to be less human is what leads to our ability to oppress and even terrorize others.

23

- When you are out and about, make the connections like Josh did—even when you don't feel comfortable doing so. I promise that each time you do so you will make wonderful discoveries that your assumptions might have otherwise obstructed. It might be something big—maybe you both believe in the power of dream interpretation to set your life course—or it might be something small—maybe you both love a certain TV series or type of cooking. In either case, the human connection will have been established.

- When you meet people, especially individuals that you perceive as being different from you with regard to a salient dimension of identity, remember to ask open-ended questions. Sometimes people lose out on making connections because of how they ask questions. For example, a white person on a ski vacation hoping to reach out to the black person she encounters on the chairlift asks, "Is this your first time skiing?" But a better question is "How often do you ski?"

- Be the one to share your interests and background first, especially if you belong to the "in group" in the dynamic. Your willingness to give of yourself makes it easier for people in the "out group" to reveal things about themselves. But don't dominate the conversation. Leave space for an even exchange.

- I'm sure you have heard of "degrees of separation." There is a cool icebreaker game that you can play with a group of people who don't know each other well. People pair up and have five minutes to find a certain number of similarities or connections between them. In some versions of the icebreaker, the pair that finds the most surprising commonality or the fewest degrees of separation wins a prize. Usually there is at least one connection that really blows one's mind. For example, person A grew up in a town where person B's mother was raised, or person B's grandfather owned a store where person A got his first bike. You might want to play this game with your group, office, or board to encourage more interaction across difference.

- Some companies survey their employees about their interests and hobbies and publish the results so that people know, for example, who plays piano, loves barbecue, or speaks Russian. One of my clients had interest fairs where people with common interests came together for an evening event, and employees visited booths exhibiting various hobbies and interests. They found that the fair enhanced their diversity goals and teamwork across status. It also created new connections for their employees, who had become very isolated in silos due to the organization's physical layout.

HABIT #5: DON'T MOURN
THE GOOD OLD DAYS
ACCEPT THAT DIVERSITY WILL
ACTUALLY LOOK AND SOUND DIFFERENT

At a cocktail party for newly matriculating students at a university, Jane, an admissions associate, and Tom, a classics professor, arrive early. As they pick up their name tags, Tom, reviewing the remaining tags, says to Jane, "Good grief, it's like the United Nations here; what ever happened to the good old days when people had simple names like *Tom* and *Jane*. I can't pronounce half these names. I know we're looking for diversity, but pretty soon we're going to be in the minority here!"

Culturally Ineffective: Wanting Everything to Stay the Same... Including Names

At first glance, some people might say, "What's the big deal? Tom is merely making a joke." As with all jokes, however, there may be profound discomfort underlying the jest. After all, many people would see the same name tags and that joke would never occur to them. Tom's comment also seems to signal that culturally he values sameness over difference. It might be a joke that reveals his discomfort with something new. He may be afraid that he won't have the skills to deal with the change that he now perceives. Consciously or unconsciously he may be resentful of the fact that more people of difference are obtaining access to opportunities and areas where people who are more like him have always been in the majority. He jokes that he is worried about becoming a minority himself, and in this way, he is admitting, whether he knows it or not, the advantage of being in the majority and a concern about how well he will fit in with an increasingly multicultural world.

Tom is also making a next-level mistake, which is assuming that Jane is like him and shares the same worldview about the school becoming more diverse. Yet Jane might actually find diversity exciting and exhilarating. She may have a life partner, child, or good friend who has a name similar to the ones that Tom judged so quickly. She may have changed her name to Jane, like many groups of people who have come to our country over the years from other lands, to blend in, allay fears, and avoid discrimination and discomfort among those like Tom who are in the majority.

If you have an easy name to pronounce, this is one of the invisible advantages that we will discuss in Habit #8, "Acknowledge Your Unearned Advantage." A recent study done in the United States, Europe, and Australia actually found that people who have names that are difficult to pronounce suffer discrimination and have a more difficult time advancing in their organizations. Another study provided research subjects with two sets of identical resumes, except in one version the applicant was given an ethnic-sounding name. The resumes with ethnic-sounding names received 50% fewer callbacks. Same resume, different names. These studies show that negative bias associated with certain names causes exclusion.

We also know that the easiest way to show inclusion and respect is to get a person's name correct. I have a name that is pronounced differently from the way people expect based on its spelling. I understand when people call me Verna (short *a* sound) rather than Vernā (Vernay) even when I tell them how to pronounce it. I don't hold it against them, but boy do I really love the people who can get it right. I just do.

Tips for Practicing This Culturally Effective Habit: Accept That Diversity Will Actually Look and Sound Different

- Don't say things like Tom did above. The old days were better for the one-up group. Now we are days of trying to create days of fairness and inclusion for all. And don't suggest that there is something wrong with the people who have names that are new to you. If we say that we support diversity, we have to accept that difference is going to look and sound different from what we have become accustomed to. Our attitude needs to be to embrace that difference even if it requires us to make adjustments and learn new skills. I have heard people remark in an unpleasant tone, "What kind of name is that?" or "Who would name someone that?" or "It would be easier for everyone if they would just shorten that name." If names are unrecognizable to you or, if, for example, you have been given the job of calling the names of graduates matriculating from your school, you could say instead, "Wow, look at all these great names—we are really making some progress reflecting our larger community. I am going to need help. Can I get the phonetic pronunciations for these names? I really want to get them right."

- If an individual has a name you don't know how to pronounce, ask the person how to say it. It's funny because some of the names that stump us are often as common to a certain nationality/ethnicity as Tom and Jane are to mainstream U.S. culture. People with names that are uncommon to us are usually happy to offer some useful mnemonic device to help you remember the correct pronunciation. Ask them to spell it while you write it down, and simply explain that you want to get it right. (You can also call someone's voicemail late at night to find out how she pronounces her own name—this is one of my favorite tricks!)

- Don't decide on your own to give someone a nickname or to abbreviate the name. Many people don't like to be called by a nickname (especially one you made up for them) at school or at work where they are trying to put their best foot forward. Nicknames are given to you by your family or your friends as a sign of affection. For people from one-down groups, naming them without their permission feels like you are taking a liberty you haven't earned, and may emphasize their one-down status. It's a small thing, but referring to a person by the name they prefer is one of the easiest ways to show respect.

- Mivoko (www.mivoko.com) is a new name-recognition software that allows employees to record the correct pronunciation of their names and have it posted on their organization's Website as well as in their signature line. Such tools will go a long way to break down discomfort and insensitivity as the students, employees, consumers, and client bases of organizations become more diverse.

- In the situation described at the beginning of this Habit, there is a bystander to Tom's comment, Jane. If Jane wants to be culturally effective, she could ask Tom one of my go-to questions when I hear something that strikes me as biased and exclusive: "What do you mean?" or "Why do you say that?" Or she could empathize and say, "I know; sometimes I also get worried that I might pronounce someone's name wrong, but I find that if I just ask them how to pronounce it, I can usually get it right. I find that most people are quite patient with me." She also might say, "I get really excited when I see these names; it means that our school is attracting talented people from all backgrounds, and that is what we need to thrive in the future." Anything a bystander can do to help the speaker or actor consider his or her comment or behavior helps to interrupt the status quo, in which biases are allowed to continue. This is the work of Habit #16, "If You See Something, Say Something."

HABIT #6: BLACK GUYS ALWAYS KNOW WHERE THEY'RE GOING
LOOK FOR YOUR BLIND SPOTS

Several years ago, my good friend Nan and I got out of a taxi late at night in the Wall Street area of New York City. Nan is Asian-American. Like me, she is a diversity consultant and former attorney. We had come from the airport and were on our way to a hotel room; as we neared our destination, our cab driver announced that there was too much construction on the street for him to take us to the front door of the hotel and it would actually be faster if we got out and walked. For some reason, we complied. If you know anything about Wall Street, it's a ghost town at night. So we stood there, bags in tow, on a dark and deserted street, not knowing exactly where to go. Then I saw this person across the street and I was immediately relieved. My friend Nan was stunned by my reaction. The person I saw was a black man. I thought, *Yeah! It's a black guy; we're saved!* But when I mentioned this to Nan later, she confided in me, "You were saying, 'Yeah! It's a black guy!' I was saying, 'Oh no, it's a black guy!'" and then she gestured running away in the other direction.

Culturally Ineffective: Allowing Blame and Shame Keep Us from Engaging with Our Blind Spots

When we got to the room the first thing Nan started to do was apologize. "I'm a woman of color and a diversity consultant and I did that whole black guy thing; I can't believe I did that. I should know better." I felt bad for her. "Look," I said, "Don't do the blame, shame thing. Think about it. I go way back with black guys: my dad is a black guy! My grandfathers were black guys. I was married to a black guy. My

6'4" son is a black guy. My world is so wide and so deep with black guys; I was pretty confident about that black guy across the street."

In my worldview, black men always know where they are going. Black men are always willing to assist as well; their chivalry comes from our deep southern roots, I think. In my mind, a black guy is exactly who I want to see when I'm lost, but Nan had much less exposure to and experience with black men. She had, as we all have, been bombarded with the negative images of black men as threatening.

Nan and I had looked at the person across the street through our lenses, the breadth and depth of our experience, and made an assessment. It was just that our lenses and our experiences were different. We were looking at the same person, yet we had completely different reactions. He was, by the way, my black guy. When I asked him if he knew where the hotel was, he replied, "Sure, I know where you ladies are going. I'll show you there." Nan was amazed!

Tips for Practicing This Culturally Effective Habit: Look for Your Blind Spots

- First understand that your way of seeing the world is just that—*your* way. It is not the only way. Get curious about what else is out there that you may not have seen.
- Be kind to yourself when you discover blind spots or the ways that you have been shaped by the *isms* on the chart on page 3. You couldn't see all the possible perspectives even if you tried. No one can.
- Don't be afraid to mix it up and try on different perspectives. Worldviews and habits of thinking are hard to break. Don't worry; if you want to return to the way you used to see and think, it will happen easily enough.
- Be patient with yourself. Again, worldviews are stubborn; it takes time for entire shifts to happen, and sometimes revelations are fleeting.

- To continue to grow and challenge your worldview, you have to get new information, and lean into rather than away from data that refutes the beliefs that you have held for a long time. One way to obtain new information is by finding new media sources.
- Hang out with people who will be honest with you and share their different views of the world without blame or shame. Use that exposure to push out your world's boundaries and eliminate the blind spots.

HABIT #7: FREAKS OF THE WEEK
SEE ALL CULTURES AS VALID

I went to China for the first time in 2006 to conduct diversity workshops with a U.S. client that had expanded to Europe and Asia. When I first arrived, the biggest shock was not the traffic; it was the staring. At first I thought I was imagining it or doing something horribly wrong and that was why everyone was peering at me. But a day into my trip, I just couldn't deny that fourteen million people seemed to be not only staring, but pointing their fingers at me. They were grabbing their children by the nape of the neck and swinging them around to face me. People would almost crash their bikes craning their necks to look at me. Yes, I was definitely on display. It did not help that I, a tall, medium-brown African-American woman with blondish super-short hair, was accompanied by a darker-skinned African-American with her hair in braids and a tall, mixed-race (Asian and white) American woman. We were the freaks of the week!

Culturally Ineffective: "Everybody Knows Staring Is Wrong... Right?"

I wish I could tell you that my first response was *Wow, a new cultural experience!* It wasn't. I was interested in taking in a new culture, of course, but I was not prepared for the way in which the new culture was taking in me. For a moment, I had forgotten everything I shared with you in Habit #3, "Be Aware of Your Own Culture and How It Shapes Your Interactions." My initial reaction instead was negative until I remembered to self-focus. I asked myself, *Why are you feeling so upset? Where did you get the idea that staring was rude?* Well, I had been taught as early as I could remember that staring was wrong. I was corrected and even reprimanded when I disobeyed this strict edict as a child. Adults around me were so serious about this standard of behavior that I assumed it was universal.

However, it wasn't just what I had been taught about staring as impolite that was the problem. I began to realize that some of my upset had to do with my African-American identity. The glaring really riled and unsettled me and brought up all sorts of feelings of fear and anger. In the United States, the history of black people and my own experience suggest that when someone who isn't black stares at a black person, it usually isn't good. The stare is a glower that communicates "Your kind of people isn't welcomed here."

What I had to remember was that I was not in the United States. I was in China, and the staring had nothing to do with the history of race relations in the United States. After closer observation, I realized that they were staring at white people with blond hair too, anyone who wasn't from China.

What I really needed to do was to understand that I was inside of a different culture. Cultures, as we discussed, have different agreed-upon norms, values, customs, beliefs, and ways of communicating that are deeply ingrained. What is intriguing is that culture operates on both a conscious and a less-conscious level, organizing our perceptions and understanding of the world in very subtle ways. People's cultures therefore make sense to them. I knew this intellectually, but at the time, I was upset. Then I realized that while many of us are interested in the cultures of others, if we are honest, we would admit that we don't necessarily consider them as legitimate or as sensible as our own. Often that is because we do not know enough to understand and appreciate the historical circumstances, experience, and context in which the culture developed. So this is the work of cultural competence—not only to see cultures and know there are differences, but to accept that every culture is valid.

Tips for Practicing This Culturally Effective Habit: See All Cultures as Valid

- Question your assumptions. If you encounter an uncomfortable dynamic that you think might be influenced by cultural difference, question your assumptions. Were the Chinese gawking only at me? No, they were staring at all sorts of foreigners. That was still not what I had been taught was proper, but it made me feel a little less singled out.
- Stay self-aware. When I was able to understand what I was bringing to the dynamic, I was able to be more objective. I had to allow for the fact that some of my upset was due to a history that wasn't China's issue. That allowed me to challenge my own interpretation of the unfolding story and to stay open to seeking out more understanding.
- Get more information. Since I wasn't able to find anything helpful in my glossy guidebooks, I mentioned my experience to a Chinese-born man who worked at one of the company's U.S. offices. I asked him to help me understand. He explained, "They've never seen anybody who looks like you before. Also, it's the summer, and many people from the countryside come to Beijing because it is the cultural center. If one lives in a big city in China, one may have seen a black person, but the folks from the countryside definitely haven't seen anyone like you." He then added, "Also, we are not taught that staring is bad or impolite." Aha! This definitely turned the tables for me. Cultural informants can be invaluable to the process of cultural effectiveness. They can help us to interpret interactions and warn us about the things to say and do and those things to avoid—all the more reason you should work on Habit #20, "Expand Your Comfort Zone and Professional and Social Circles." The very next day after the dinner with my Chinese cultural informant, I went outside

my westernized hotel and when people stared, I smiled and waved, not wildly, just a small wave. To my surprise, they smiled too and waved back!

- Ultimately, I learned that to be culturally competent, one needs to spend much more time learning about the culture of the country that you plan to visit. It is a sign of cultural superiority actually to plop down in a completely different country and expect to be comfortable and attended in accordance to one's own ways of being. And one would not only look at the objective aspects of the culture like temples, dress, and food. One would learn about those more subjective aspects of the culture such as beliefs, values, and history ideas with the mindset that all cultures are equally valid.

HABIT #8: TAKE THE OPPORTUNITY WALK
ACKNOWLEDGE YOUR UNEARNED ADVANTAGES

When we have the right space and group composition, I ask people to take the Opportunity Walk with their colleagues. To start, I ask everyone in the group to create a line, shoulder to shoulder, stretching across the width of the room; everyone is starting at the same place. I then ask various questions, and depending on their answers people step forward or back. The typical questions are: *If your ancestors were forced against their will to come to the United States, step back. If most of your family members worked in careers requiring college education, step forward. If you ever tried to change your appearance, behavior, or speech to avoid being judged on the basis of the perception other people had of your race, ethnicity, religion, or sexual orientation, step back. If your family owned its own house, step forward. If the head of your organization is of the same race/ethnicity as you are, step forward.* You get the idea.

At the end of the exercise, I stand in front of the group and hold up a fresh twenty-dollar bill. I tell them that it represents a valuable opportunity and that the person who gets to me first after I count to three can have the twenty dollars. Despite the fact that we all started off the exercise in the same place, at this point there are some people right in front of my face because of the steps that they have taken forward, and some are way in the back. No matter how fast or capable those in the back rows are, at the count of three, they will not be able to get to the twenty-dollar bill before those at the front.

Culturally Ineffective: Thinking You Hit a Triple

The overall message of this metaphorical walk is clear: The life circumstances in which we find ourselves—the unearned advantages we inherited—position some of us better than others to take advantage of opportunity. These advantages have nothing to do with what we earned or merited, but rather result from an old system that favored and positioned one group over another. Remember the chart we studied in Habit #1 that helped us examine this system? It's consistent with an old expression: *He was born on third base and went through life thinking he hit a triple.*

As you can imagine, people have many different reactions to the walk, and most are deeply moved by their experience of revisiting the events of their lives and using it to consider what got them where they are today. Obviously you can quibble with the questions and whether a particular question should entitle a person to move backward or forward. However, the visual of the group starting all together in the same place and then breaking ranks as the questions sort them is profound. The whole group is moving constantly, but each person is taking a personal journey through time, considering what the questions mean in his or her own life and how he or she compares to others.

Those who end up in the front of the room at the end of the opportunity walk usually talk about feeling guilty and shortening their steps near the end because they are so far ahead of others. But I remind them that there is no reason to feel guilty. The exercise is not about anything they did; it is about *unearned* advantages. The walk demonstrates the privileges that existed before they were even born, or resulted from the actions of others (parents, government, community, religious institutions), over which they had no control. While this is true, what remains for them and for each of us is to acknowledge the unearned advantage into which we have come. If we do not see the way the old-fashioned systems of oppression and privilege unfairly give us a leg up in certain situations and opportunities within our workplaces and societies, we will overvalue our worth and those of other one-up groups. We will also underestimate the value of others in one-down groups to our workplaces, communities, and organizations.

One of the most difficult aspects about being culturally effective in this area is that unearned advantages are often invisible to the untrained eye. It is also easier to see when individuals are being treated unfairly or are at a disadvantage because of their one-down classifications than to see when we are being treated more favorably because of a difference. Privilege is the other side of the coin of disadvantage.

I remember when I first came to the realization of unearned privilege in my life. I knew quite well the advantage of being a woman, and an African-American from a humble background, but I hadn't spent one moment noticing the way the world was so much easier for me because I was Protestant, straight, U.S. born, educated in elite schools, and without disabilities. That's a long list of advantages, and I hadn't even detected them! But once you start looking for the places in your daily life where there is no friction and things are smooth—the places where you are a "fish in water"—you can discover them, big and small, everywhere.

Unearned advantage is the same as being on the return leg of a flight from San Francisco on its way to Boston. When you leave from the East Coast, the pilot announces it will take six and a half hours, but when you are coming back you are told it will take only four and a half or five hours. It's the same distance and route. What accounts for the difference? Headwinds and tailwinds! Unearned advantage is like a tailwind, an invisible force that assists the movement of the one-up group. Those in the one-up group may be working hard, but their hard work is made easier and faster by the tailwind of privilege. But when that plane is headed across the country in the face of headwinds, it doesn't matter how great the plane is and how hard it is working, the headwinds are an external force that creates difficulty and slows down the effort. This is true for members of the one-down group; they encounter external forces that impede their momentum. They may arrive ultimately, but it's a very different effort and journey.

41

Once you see that you are the recipient of unearned advantage in your life, it is disorienting, especially if you were taught that all you have accomplished and all that others have and have not achieved are due to individual hard work and merit. These revelations require you to change the way you see the world and your role in it. It can be hard to accept this different view or figure out what to do with this new information. You may be tempted to fall back into your old way of thinking and to put the blinders back on.

In order for someone to be down, someone else has to be up. Culturally effective people work hard to keep conscious of the uncomfortable truth that in some situations they are in the front of the Opportunity Walk line. Because they know that by doing so, they can use their advantaged position to create positive change for those behind them.

Tips for Practicing This Culturally Effective Habit: Acknowledge Your Unearned Advantages

- Stay conscious despite any destabilizing revelations about privilege you might experience; when you know you have unearned advantages, you can use to them to contribute to inclusion and equity in ways that you couldn't before you realized these advantages. Knowledge is power!
- Accepting our unearned advantage is an act of courage. Accepting our unearned advantage—without guilt—makes it easier to use the Habits in this book. Just remind yourself: this new awareness is about low guilt, high responsibility.
- Study the one-up designations on the chart on page 3, and become familiar with ways that you have received the benefit of the doubt simply because you belong to a particular group. Charts like these can help us see the privileges

we have inherited that we might overlook because we are comfortable and in sync with our dominant culture.

- Make a distinction between unearned advantage and undeserved advantage. Being a member of several privileged groups (such as being able-bodied, being a Protestant, or being educated at the nation's top schools) doesn't mean that we haven't worked hard. It may mean that we have worked *as hard* as someone who is from several undervalued groups, yet we may have gotten appreciably further, faster, and with less friction than them.
- Start paying attention to how unearned privilege works in your life. Make a list of your unearned advantages and how they have assisted you in your life journey. Look for something small and less consequential at first. For example, when you go to a store to find a greeting card, how many cards show fathers, mothers, babies, and scenes that reflect your race/ethnicity, family structure, religion, etc.? Or when you walk into your hotel room, what music is playing—music you love or least enjoy? Next, look at things that have more of an impact. When you walk into your office, for example, do most of the people share your race and gender? Do the leaders? When you walk in a store and are professionally dressed, are you free to stroll and browse without suspicion or anyone following you? Do you experience kind smiles and assistance? When you do well on a project, are you expected to do so or is your performance met with surprise? Do people see you as a credit to your one-down group? Finally, consider larger questions, of the greatest impact. What have been your experiences with law enforcement and the legal system? Are you able to live in a safe neighborhood with good schools with others who share your racial/ethnic identity? Is your advancement thwarted by sexual harassment by your boss? Have you lost a job or been denied a promotion

43

because of your parental obligations or marital status? Is your patriotism ever questioned by people who don't know you? Do you ever fear harm from others because of your sexual orientation or religion?

- Realize that we may have very different life experiences than our colleagues. While we may be working in the same institution, for example, people may have taken very different and more difficult paths to get there. As a result, their perceptions of and comfort level in the workplace may be very different.

- Start looking at the ways that privilege has been embedded in the organizations of which you are a part. Can you see practices and policies where certain people receive the benefit of the doubt because their group is automatically perceived as better than (e.g., more moral, smarter, more trustworthy, etc.)? These advantages might be extended when individuals are hired, or when decisions are made for promotion. This analysis is the first step in bias-proofing your organizations which we talk about extensively in the last chapter of *Moving Diversity Forward*. The next step is to revise your policies and practices so they level the playing field and provide equal access to opportunity. This is the only way to support success of people of the one-down group as well as the institution itself.

44

HABIT #9: TAKE PEOPLE OUT OF THE BOXES YOU PUT THEM IN
RESIST ELITISM AND EMBRACE HUMAN VALUE

I was part of a group that had gathered to do an environmental cleanup of a beach and the surrounding grounds. Some people were asked to help erect a ramp so that those with wheelchairs could have access to the beach. Some people were asked to paint the lifeguard chairs with beautiful bright colors. My group was assigned to pick up trash. *Bummer! Not a great use of my skills,* I thought, but I complied because it would be unseemly to complain about the job I was assigned to do on a "do good" day.

Someone from the Metropolitan District Commission (referred to as MDC, the parks and recreation department for Boston) led our group. This guy had arrived at the beach in his pickup truck, and he was wearing his MDC work gear: matching dark shirt and pants with his name over the shirt pocket. He wore a hat, had a beard, and was white and middle-aged. As he led us through the part of the beach with trees and bushes, I obediently picked up discarded cups and paper. Then he told us about the park and pointed out its beauty. He asked us to listen closely to the birds in the trees overhead. Using their calls, he identified the different types of birds. He talked about the fish and the turtles in the nearby waterways and the technology used to keep the waterways clean, including the processes he had learned while working on a project in Africa. I thought to myself, *GOTCHA!*

Culturally Ineffective: Being Elitist and Putting People in a Box

I was shocked—and then embarrassed by how shocked I was—because this man was so interesting, so smart and knew things about which I knew nothing. *Thank goodness, he can't read my mind!* I thought. How did I get myself into this situation? Because when I saw this guy I had immediately put him into a box: the MDC guy box.

In that box, I had decided certain things about him: he had limited education; he was not very progressive; he liked sports, beer, football…. in other words, I had made him out to be "less than" based on his job status, appearance, uniform, and truck. Yes, you can find my misguided thinking on the chart on page 3. It is called "elitism." In the events that ensued, he had broken so far out of this box that it was clear I had constructed one. I had been cordial to this guy, not disrespectful in any way (thank goodness!)—but that was different from being respectful in the sense that I respected or expected the value that he could bring to my life.

After I returned home from the beach that day, I thought about all the people I may have missed along the way. What if I stayed open to the signal that I was putting someone in a box, and moved towards them instead of being content to label them and leave them alone? How much richer and more unexpected would my life become?

We make assumptions all the time about who people are, what they are interested in, and what they have to offer. Even if the MDC guy had been the person I initially constructed and fit neatly into my box, he would have undoubtedly enhanced my life in some way, if I was able to lay down my superiority and authentically engage with him. The scientists say the assumptions we make happen because this is how our brains naturally organize and deal with the constant stimuli that come at us. We immediately categorize people into "in groups" (people like us) and "out groups" (people unlike us). It's automatic, so often we don't realize that we are making assumptions. Instead, for efficiency's sake, we believe the stories that our brains have concocted.

I also see evidence of these boxes in the companies with which I work. Often when senior people talk to administrative staff, they reveal they don't see those in certain administrative positions as equals; in other words, senior people have put administrative staff in a box. Once an administrative assistant said that her boss had tickets to a classical music concert that he couldn't attend and wanted to find someone to take them off his hands. He asked her to call around to other directors to see if anyone wanted them, but ultimately she was unsuccessful. When he raised his hands in exasperation because no one could use the tickets, she asked if she could have them. He replied, "What? You? I didn't think you liked classical music." She informed him that she indeed loved classical music. Why didn't he think she liked classical music? Was it because he had her in a socioeconomic class box based on what she did for a living, and somehow that box didn't have classical music in it?

47

Tips for Practicing This Culturally Effective Habit: Resist Elitism and Embrace Human Value

- Continue to be cordial and kind. As we have said, nice alone is not enough to move diversity forward, but it's a start. And it's certainly preferable to the disregard we sometimes show to people we encounter.
- What if, instead of my putting the MDC guy in his box, I had assumed that he was a valuable part of my journey and could enrich my life? An assumption like this one helps diversity move forward. Remember how much you hate it when people "box" you in and, as a result, mistreat or ignore you.
- Pay attention to any and all conversations that you have with people you don't know well or at all. (These could be exchanges at work, in an interview, at a meeting at your child's school, or even on an airplane or in a coffee shop.) If you keep a mental record of what you notice, I'll bet those observations will

yield new and surprising information about the types of boxes you create for people, and the types of people you often put in those boxes. Ask yourself where you learned what goes in these boxes and how you can unlearn it.

- Listening, observing—and above all, relaxing—in someone else's presence allows us to show respect and reflect not just on new information, but on the presence of our edges, our bounded assumptions.

- If you don't want to say the wrong thing, pause before you speak—which seems so obvious! Yet it was crucial that day on the beach. Just the act of holding my tongue until my revealing and embarrassing assumptions were challenged, was a lifesaver.

- To do all the above, you will need to let go of your sense of superiority. I know most of us don't go around thinking we are better than other people, but sometimes there can be no other explanation for why we warm up to some folks and completely shun others. We may be cordial but it's in an arms-length kind of way. I am asking you to move closer to those in the one-down group across from you on the chart on page 3. In other words, break through the boxes that are the foundation for the chart.

- Once you realize that people don't belong in the box, then what? Instead of only saying hello and smiling, why not introduce yourself? Tell people your name, ask theirs, look for the commonalities, appreciate the differences, and expect richness. In other words, follow the habits in this book.

HABIT #10: PAY ATTENTION TO
THE BATHROOMS
REAL INCLUSION IS IN THE DETAILS

When the first group of women matriculated to Harvard Law School in 1953, they were completely surprised that when they arrived at the ivy halls of the law school, there were no bathrooms for the women! As smart law school students, they argued to school administrators that requiring them to walk to Harvard Square (a good ten- to fifteen-minute walk) to use the restroom was unfair, since their male counterparts did not have to do the same. How would they make it to their classes on time? What would they do if they had to use the restroom during class or a test? The men at Harvard decided they had a point, and they installed a toilet in the janitor's closet in the basement of a large classroom building. That is where these fantastically brilliant women were relegated when they needed to use the bathroom.

Culturally Ineffective: "I Want Difference, But I Don't Want to Have To Do Anything Differently"

In 1953 Harvard Law School had gender diversity but not gender inclusion. Diversity is about who is represented in the organization, whereas inclusion speaks more to who is respected, expected, and integrated into an institution. Diversity may be the conscious message that your organization or community is sending, but the lack of inclusion can easily and sometimes unconsciously communicate a contrary message. In the Harvard Law School example, without something as basic as a women's bathroom, would those women be crazy to conclude that the powers that be didn't want them there? At the least, they might imagine that the institution did not understand, respect, or see them.

It's really hard to know how to include others if you are well established and reflected in an institution. It is the classic fish-in-water problem. It's hard to see who's been left out when you feel completely left in. This is one of the costs of being in the one-up group. After all, when the men of Harvard Law School got the urge to relieve themselves, they walked down the hall. It only makes sense that those who begin an organization, structure that organization in a way that reflects their needs, values, and worldview. To build an organization, team, or community that is culturally effective it has to change some of the ways it used to do things. It's extremely hard for the ingroup to make this shift by itself. Those in power will have to partner with and begin to value the people from the one-down group who have been historically marginalized and excluded from the institution, community, neighborhood, or organization.

Once you have included a more diverse group of people, the next task is to learn how to draw them out so that you and your effort can benefit from their inclusion. You may need to learn unthreatening ways to ask for input from newcomers who have come on board. The power of inclusion is allowing these differences to flourish in a way that enhances the organization's or team's performance.

As I like to say, "Diversity is being invited to the party; inclusion is being asked to dance."

After you have included people and made them feel comfortable enough to express themselves, how about using your unearned advantage in a given situation to make a further difference? In other words, you will need to help remove the structural impediments to their inclusion, i.e., install some new toilets.

Tips for Practicing This Culturally Effective Habit: Real Inclusion Is in the Details

- Ask for input from others. Are there administrators, program coordinators, parents, presidents, or directors in other institutions who have implemented successful diversity and inclusion efforts recently? Are there specific steps they took or things they wished they had known that can now benefit your diversity and inclusion initiatives?

- Think about when you first came to the organization or neighborhood. Did you feel welcome? If so, what made you feel welcome? Despite your present level of comfort, these questions might help you remember that it wasn't always that way and may give you a concrete idea of what to do or not to do with others who are orienting to the new environment.

- Consult others in your institution who may have been swimming upstream at one point in the organization's history. What groups of people used to be underrepresented in your institution because of religion, ethnicity, disability, age, or language? They may have insight about what made them feel included when they entered, or what they wished had been done to make them feel more accepted and integrated.

- Invite the new or underrepresented group to be part of the orientation process. What do they want to know? What do they need? How can you and the organization be responsive? How do you keep the communication open and flowing?

- Don't make the mistake of assuming that everyone communicates or makes contributions the same way. Notice who's not talking when you ask, "Does anyone have anything to add?" Many people, especially when they are not well represented in an environment, are reluctant to speak out. They don't want to be perceived as troublemakers or not good team players. Employ different strategies to solicit opinion and ideas (e.g., round-robins where everyone takes a turn, using secret ballots or a suggestion box, writing thoughts and questions on index cards anonymously, soliciting information before and after meetings in person and via telephone or e-mail). When new ideas are offered, make sure that you respond in a way that encourages more input.

- For organizations: undertake a cultural audit or assessment. Have a third party conduct confidential interviews, focus groups, and surveys of those in the organization to determine how they are experiencing the workplace. How are individuals from one-down groups faring? For example, how are the company's policies and practices (formal and informal systems or structures) affecting racial minorities, as compared to whites in the environment or women as compared to men or baby boomers as compared to millennials? Ask people who are well represented in the organization about their experiences and opportunities, too, so that you can get a complete picture and compare how your practices are affecting everyone.

HABIT #11: HOW ARE WE SUPPOSED
TO TELL THEM APART?
MAKE THE EFFORT TO REALLY SEE A PERSON

Ty (short for Taeyang), a young Asian man, told me that he was in his law firm's cafeteria when a partner at the firm came up to him and quickly and emphatically instructed him to contact a client regarding an urgent matter. Ty, who wasn't an attorney, but a scientist in the firm's patent department, was so confused by the situation as it was unfolding that only after the partner had left did he realize what had happened. The partner had mistaken him for someone else. He hurried to his office and telephoned Jason, the one Asian male lawyer in the litigation department and tried his best to convey the partner's message. Jason recognized that it was a partner he was working with, but after the call Jason still wasn't certain about what the partner wanted him to do. So Jason, in the most pleasant way possible, called the partner, explained that he knew some urgent matter needed his immediate attention, but that he was not the one in the cafeteria with whom the partner had communicated. The partner apologized; the associate assured him that it was no big deal and that he was only calling to find out what to do.

Culturally Ineffective: Being Oblivious to Difference and Adding Insult to Injury

When some white people make a mistake that involves a person of color, they feel so mortified, that even if they are not afraid of being sued they stop talking or trying to engage with the other person. After the day of the mix-up in the cafeteria, Jason saw the partner's behavior toward him change: the partner seemed to avoid one-on-one meetings with him, and when he saw the partner, the partner would never look him in the eye. He also never received any other work from that partner after the matter closed. Perhaps the partner withdrew because he was embarrassed; by doing so, however, he compounded to his error and the impact of such an event on Jason, who was now worried about his opportunities for success in that environment.

Another client told me about a situation in which a working group contained several Asian women who were constantly being misidentified by their managers. They were receiving each other's e-mail and phone calls as well. The women came to the company's Diversity Director because they were worried that people might be confused enough to make errors when deciding on their work opportunities or evaluating their work performances. When the Director spoke to the managers about the problem, several of the managers said, "How are we supposed to tell them apart?"

We know that mistaken identity happens to everyone, but it is more likely to happen when people are underrepresented in a particular setting. The brain just starts clumping individuals into one group based on physical appearance. It might happen to the two redheads in the division or the two young men if most of the men are older. In my consulting practice we call it conspicuous invisibility when minority people stick out because of their group identity but are invisible when it comes to their identities as individual people.

This happens frequently to Asians because some people in the certain parts of the United States have not spent much time living or working with people of Asian heritage. There are also several studies that suggest Asian-Americans (Asian-Pacific Islanders and South Asian) are still thought of as foreign, even though they may have grown up in New York or Kansas City and speak non-accented English. Many Asian-Americans talk about this conspicuous invisibility in their workplace. The impact of being invisible is that they are not included in certain opportunities or activities. People just don't think of them or don't see them as the go-to person.

Conspicuous invisibility is especially difficult to endure in a workplace, group, or committee where individuals from a one-down group are trying to believe that success is possible, even though the composition of the upper echelons of the company offers very little proof of such. If they look up the chain of command and see very few people who look like them, they begin to conclude that their prospects for success in the environment are doubtful. Unless they have solid opportunities or relationships with the majority or one-up group in the organization, they will often start to disengage from the organization and make plans to try their luck elsewhere. Or they will stay put, but withdraw and adopt a strategy of doing just enough to get by. I have seen this attitude among many employees who are racial or ethnic minorities, and it's something I refer to as protective disengagement.

Tips for Practicing This Culturally Effective Habit: Make the Effort to Really See a Person

- What if the partner who mistook Jason, the Asian associate, decided as a result of the mix-up to make sure that he actually visited Jason's office, invited him to lunch, and worked with him on another project? As you will see in Habit #19, when you use your mistakes as a learning opportunity, in many cases, you can catapult relationships further forward than if there had been no mix-up whatsoever.
- Understand that this type of mistake is not about racism, but if it continues or if you throw your hands up and don't try to fix the mistake or get better at distinguishing faces of people of color, your inaction is rooted in racism because you are avoiding the work of building authentic relationships across race. After all, you avoid a group of people only if you think there is no value to having them in your personal or work life in a genuine way. You have to make the effort if you are going to change the outcome.

- To prevent future mistakes, in addition to expanding the relationship with Jason, the partner in question could spend a little time with the company directory. Most companies have electronic facebooks (in the original sense) where you can study the names and faces of individuals with whom you are likely to have contact.

- Be on guard outside of the workplace, like a gym or your kids' school, or in situations where there likely is no directory that matches names with faces. Take the time to look at the person that you meet. I will actually say to myself, *Okay, pay attention to this person because your brain is going to try to group him with the few other folks here who have a similar physical appearance with nothing to distinguish them.* Find out more about the person so that you can use one of those mnemonic devices to remember someone's name based on something individual to the person.

- If you are in an organization, you might want to do what one of my clients did once they were comfortable with the idea that they were committed to the sometimes bumpy journey of diversity and inclusion. They approved a funny skit that the new class of attorneys created in which the joke centered on several new black male associates being called by each other's names. At the end of the skit, the black associates who had helped develop the skit good-naturedly stood side by side along with several other black men who were not new to the firm, and each man introduced himself. They were calling out the problem with humor, offering understanding and a solution. *Warning:* this kind of humor works only in certain situations: an institution has made diversity discussable; and the architects of the skit include prominent and respected people from the underrepresented or one-down group.

HABIT #12: SHE WAS SO ARTICULATE
AVOID MICRO-INEQUITIES

My friend, Jada, went to see the former U.S. Secretary of State Condeleeza Rice give a book talk. Jada, who is black, ran into a white colleague she knew well in the bookstore cafe following the reading. The first comment that her acquaintance made, in a tone that indicated surprise, was that she was impressed that Rice was so articulate. Jada thought of all the things that were on her mind about Rice's presentation; Rice's ability to express herself forcefully and eloquently was certainly not on the list! After all, she had been President Bush's National Security Advisor—the first woman to hold that position. She had been provost at Stanford and, in addition to English, speaks four languages, including German and Russian. How could she be anything but articulate?

Culturally Ineffective: "With Compliments Like That, Who Needs Enemies?"

What could be possibly wrong with saying a person was articulate? It was a compliment! True, but the harder question is did Jada's white colleague express surprise at how articulate Rice was because she expected Rice to be less than an excellent public speaker? And was that assumption perhaps based on Rice's racial heritage or gender? Is *articulate* a term that she would use with a white male national security advisor? And would she have been surprised? Who knows? What I do know is that sometimes we have to watch our compliments, because they betray the negative perceptions that we harbor about a person based on the person's group identity rather than who the person is and what he or she has done as an individual. This type of compliment is an example of what we call micro-inequities.

Let me give you another example of a micro-inequity so you can see what I mean. A colleague was appointed as the head of a large important organization and was meeting her entire board for the first time. The president of the board stood up and introduced her by sharing with the board all of her professional accomplishments, education, and awards. A white male member of board who was sitting beside her leaned over after hearing her bio and said, "Even if you never did another thing, for a black girl you have really done a lot."

A micro-inequity, sometimes also called a micro-insult or micro-aggression, is a quick, small act that results in a slight or an indignity. One might state an assumption about a young married woman's lack of long-term commitment to the organization, or offhandedly question the work ethic of a person who wasn't born in this country. One might confuse someone from a one-down racial group with another individual from his or her race or assume that the person is an assistant when he or she is, in fact, the Vice President. One might forget to introduce someone from a one-down group to an important client or notice and reward the accomplishment of someone from a one-up group and fail to do the same for an equally deserving member of the team who is from a one-down group.

A micro-inequity can be a remark or even a glance or tone of voice. It may be intentional, but many times it is not. Even when such acts are unintentional, however, they reveal a negative or erroneous assumption by the member of the one-up group about the one-down group. An example of this might be using the word *qualified* only when describing a candidate you are seeking to hire from a one-down group, but not from a one-up group. Sometimes gay people hear "You don't seem gay to me; I mean you seem so normal." Sometimes Asian-Americans tell me that people who don't know anything about them might comment at work, "Your English is very good; when did you come to the country?"

Because such acts are small and often subtle, they are hard to talk about or correct. The common excuse offered for micro-inequities is that they are insignificant, and "We don't want to be walking on eggshells around here." A person who commits a micro-inequity might go on the defensive saying, "Can't we tell a joke anymore? Everyone's so serious!" Yet the effect of micro-inequities is real—they create irritation, frustration, and anger. When they happen over and over again, they accumulate and develop a weight of their own. Some people liken it to bleeding to death because of a thousand tiny paper cuts. Micro-inequities can make talented and capable employees question whether they can do their best or be successful in such an environment and may contribute to a desire to leave the organization.

Tips for Practicing This Culturally Effective Habit: Avoid Micro-Inequities

- Think before you speak, especially when you are telling a joke. Is it at someone else's expense? Things that we used to think were funny, were only funny because no one at the table represented the group we were putting down. Thanks to the work of increased diversity, chances are that there are different individuals at the table now with different sensibilities and sensitivities.
- Understand the difference between intent and impact. The hardest thing to appreciate fully is how often micro-inequities happen, whether consciously or unconsciously, and how exhausting it is for people who have to deal with them. If you can spend a little time considering how needling and frustrating it is to hear these slights repeatedly from different people, you may work harder to develop a more multi-dimensional understanding of individuals who are from groups different from your own.
- Sometimes the people who are guilty of micro-inequities are well meaning

WHAT IF I SAY THE WRONG THING: 25 HABITS FOR CULTURALLY EFFECTIVE PEOPLE

and might even think of themselves as cool, for example, people who decide to use certain slang expressions only with and always with individuals from a one-down group because they think by using the venacular, they are bonding with the individuals in the group. Really they are offending them. Challenge them—and yourself—to really be cool by communicating that you want to know when you are using the wrong language or making it uncomfortable for people of difference to be around you. Make it clear that if you are corrected, you won't hold it against the person you insulted and you won't insist on talking only about your intent while refusing to appreciate the impact of your actions.

- Pay attention to a person's reaction when you make a comment. If you feel the tenor of the conversation change or the individual withdraw from the conversation, just ask the person if you said something that was wrong or offensive. Often that person will reply halfheartedly that everything is okay; they may be more forthcoming if you say something like "I'm really trying to figure out when I am putting my foot in my mouth so that I can stop doing it. If you could help me, I would appreciate it."

- Organizations and individuals can start using the term micro-inequities and teaching people what they are. A very prominent corporate trainer, Steven Young, has a great interactive training on micro-messaging that helps people to explore the subject. When people have the vocabulary and engage in dialogue about micro-inequities they can start pointing out these subtle but impactful actions and changing these behaviors in themselves and others when they see them. Then they are prepared to take on the tips in Habit #21, "Being Proactive Doesn't Mean Taking A Second Job."

HABIT #13: ARE YOU SURE YOU'RE A DOCTOR?
CHALLENGE YOUR DESCRIPTIVE BIAS

Years ago, I had been up all night nursing my sick child. I was in a frenzy by the time we arrived at his doctor's office early the next morning. My child's regular physician wasn't there. A young, petite South Asian woman wearing a white coat and a stethoscope around her neck walked into the exam room. She introduced herself to me as the doctor. Without knowing what I was doing, I started questioning her: "So, have you ever taken care of kids with these symptoms before? How many?" She spoke with an Indian accent, so when she answered my questions, I would add in a raised voice, "What? I don't know what you are saying." It was like I was a member of a medical licensing board and thought she was lying about being a doctor—I treated her as if she were an impostor.

Culturally Ineffective: "You Don't Match the Picture in My Head"
Yes, this type of situation happens even to those of us who have been extensively trained in diversity and inclusion work! When I am brave enough to share this story with people, they try to excuse my behavior by suggesting that I was not myself: my son was sick, and I had been up all night. This is true, and it is also true that our automatic responses get the best of us when we are in difficult situations, but nonetheless, it was still bias that informed my behavior. I treated the doctor this way because she was a young Asian woman; her youth and diminutive stature brought up additional biases for me. If a white man had walked into that room, even without a stethoscope or introduction, I would have immediately felt at ease, like I was in the right place with the right person—and in good hands. If it had been a black woman, I am sure I would have been at least friendlier and more trusting. Yet, my

61

automatic response to this South Asian woman was that she wasn't qualified to take care of my son.

A response like mine is what we call descriptive bias. We have a picture in our heads of what a doctor, a leader, an astronaut, or even a president should look like based on years of seeing only one group in this position due to the historical exclusion of others. We have also been told which one-up group is better or smarter or more reliable than another. Over a long time, sexist and racist ideas get embedded in our psyche, and they are also reflected and reinforced everyday in the media. In addition, complex institutional barriers that we talked about in Habit #1, "But I'm Not a Racist," informed by biased ways of thinking, often unacknowledged, thwart those in the one-down group from being well represented in professional positions. When my son's doctor came in looking as she did, I didn't see a doctor because unconsciously for me, a doctor was a man. Thank goodness, many of these pictures that our brains are taking in from the media and in school are changing, but old mental associations die a hard death.

Have you heard the riddle about a young man and his father who were severely injured in a traffic accident? Tragically, the father died and the young man was rushed to the hospital. When the surgeon came into the operating room and saw the young man, the surgeon said, "I cannot operate on this boy; this boy is my son." Who was the surgeon? I can't tell you how many people make these hypotheses: the young man was adopted by two gay guys, or the patient was the surgeon's stepson and the father who died was the biological father or vice-versa. Some people even suggest that maybe the "father" who died in the car accident was a priest, not a real father. Most people are stuck for a few minutes before they can get their brains to go to the possibility that the surgeon was a woman.

This kind of descriptive bias becomes a huge problem when it comes to advancement and leadership. We know for the most part that we shouldn't discriminate against any group in the hiring context, but often descriptive bias affects the more subjective promotion process. Decision makers may be unaware that often they are looking for someone who fits their in-group because their description of a leader is someone from that group. For example, men alone were allowed to be leaders for so long that now when we define leadership, we often define it through the lens of gender. We frequently rely on the more traditional male-like attributes of agency (assertive, individualistic, dominant, self-reliant, and ambitious) to judge who will be a good leader instead of developing criteria that speak to the genuine and evolving competencies of effective leadership. Studies on leadership suggest that the best leaders have the attributes of agency tempered with the communal qualities that have traditionally been associated with women: interpersonal, supportive, kind, and empathetic.

Tips for Practicing This Culturally Effective Habit: Challenge Your Descriptive Bias

- When you realize that you are in the middle of interrogating someone who may be from a one-down group, the first thing to do is examine your body language. Instead of leaning back on your heels, relax your body posture. If your arms are folded in front of your body, uncross them and soften your stare. When you make these simple postural adjustments, it is easier to start listening instead of questioning. When you do speak, see if you can use a warmer tone, one that isn't quite so stern. Once I pulled back from my descriptive bias with the doctor and adjusted my body poster, I realized she was quite wonderful and competent. By the end of the interaction, I was a real fan and sorry I had acted so foolishly.

- To broaden the picture of whom can competently perform various roles traditionally dominated by only one group, talk to yourself; tell yourself this is a wonderful way to erase negative stereotypical thinking. In my situation with the doctor, I might say to myself something like this: *You believe that people of every background are smart and competent. She stated that she was a doctor. She has on a white coat. She is working at this reputable institution. There is no reason to doubt that she is a highly capable doctor. Now, stop it!*

- Once you recover from the bad direction you might have been going in when you encountered a person who challenged your descriptive bias, make sure the other person knows how much you appreciate them, either by smiling, thanking them, or offering compliments.

- For organizations: Examine your criteria of advancement and leadership, even for high-level entry positions. Are you overvaluing male-like attributes? Have you looked closely at the type of competencies that are effective in each position? How did you determine this? If you are looking only at people who have been successful in the past, you might be replicating a narrow view of leadership and missing out on the great talent that can help lead you into the future. Also acknowledge the downside of your present leadership. What's missing? If you have lots of talented women, people of color, LGBT individuals, and other underrepresented minorities at the bottom of your organization but very few in your senior ranks, descriptive bias may be getting in the way.

HABIT #14: YOU DON'T SOUND LIKE A COP
BECOME MUTUALLY ADAPTIVE

Sandra is an Asian-American police detective, brought on to the force to help with an outbreak of crime in the town's large Vietnamese population. She has made great inroads into various complicated problems by earning the trust of local business owners with broad roots in the community. People in the precinct find her pleasant to work with, and she has consistently delivered timely and reliable information. However, she is now working on a high-profile case with John, an inspector, and she is concerned. Every time she meets or talks with John on the telephone, he barks at her that he can't hear her, that she is speaking too softly.

Recently, John leaves a voice mail for Sandra; at the end of the message, he remarks that she should change her outgoing message because she doesn't sound tough enough to be a cop. He adds, "If you plan to be successful in this profession, you need to learn how to deepen your voice." Sandra is not sure what she should do. Should she change her demeanor to please John? Should she stick with her natural ways of expression, which, although it is receptive and encouraging, it is far from soft and has proved successful to this point?

Culturally Ineffective: "We Let Them in; Now It's Up to Them to Figure Out How to Fit In"

When organizations and individuals say they are committed to diversity, they are not always aware of what attitudes are required to grow diversity. It is not enough to invite difference, you have to recognize that difference makes a difference. Maybe it is with regard to something obvious, such as the different names described in Habit #5, "Don't Mourn The Good Old Days" or an individual's accent, dress, or hairstyle.

But it also means being able to appreciate that people have different values, world-views, and ways of interacting and communicating.

As we mentioned in Habit #3, "Be Aware of Your Own Culture and How It Shapes Your Interactions," some of how we present ourselves has to do with how we were raised—our cultural norms—some, with our personality, and some, with how we have been socialized. Sandra has demonstrated her capabilities; she has succeeded in part because the exact style of personal presentation that John finds anathema is familiar to her community. Sandra is being judged inadequate by John because he believes his style is the only way to communicate. While Sandra can make some adjustments to interact with individuals like John who have different presentation syle, John is missing a chance to be mutually adaptive. He may think he is being helpful to Sandra by telling her what it takes, but much of this has to do with his attitude and lack of cultural fluency.

If we want women to flourish in the workplace, we can't have an environment that works only for the narrowest group of women, those who have more male-like attributes. If we want people of color to be effective, we can't ask them to interact only in accordance with the norms and values of Western European culture and deny the ways of being that are more aligned with their culture. If we want LGBT people to be comfortable in our communities, we can't insist that they act straight or not talk about their lives with their same-sex partners. If we want millennials to make contributions to our organizations, we can't insist that they operate in the same way baby boomers do. In other words, we can't say we want difference and then ask people who are different from the dominant group to do their best impression of those who are already in the majority. Why? Because people like Sandra will feel uncomfortable if we insist that they change who they are or cover what makes them different and adopt the same values and manner-*isms* of the dominant culture. This discomfort often causes to them to be less productive or less committed to the organization, and then they leave. Just as troubling, we will miss out on the power of diversity. We won't have the benefit of the different perspectives and approaches that allow groups to better solve problems and make more accurate predictions. Our business, nonprofit, and faith communities won't be as prosperous and relevant, and our personal lives will not be as rich.

Dr. Mitch Hammer created a survey called the Intercultural Development Inventory (IDI), based on the work of Dr. Milton Bennett. Many individuals and groups have taken the IDI, and the majority of people (68%), no matter how progressive they think they are on diversity issues, remain in the minimization stage. People in this stage essentially care about fairness but don't understand that working with people of different cultures requires changes in how rules and norms are applied to different groups. They see difference, but they don't want it to matter. Some of us are accepting of difference but we don't have the skills to be adaptive. Becoming mutually adaptive means that we not only value difference but we are able to see ways that our organization and its individuals can change practices and mores to respect and take advantage of difference. Intercultural competence is developmental and aspirational in that none of us are perfectively adaptive to all cultural differences. We will always be learning to interact with cultural differences more effectively.

Tips for Practicing This Culturally Effective Habit: Become Mutually Adaptive

- It is important to understand not only the objective forms of different cultures (e.g., dress, music, artistic expression, food) but also the subjective forms of culture, such as agreed-upon values and expectations and the ways groups regard hierarchy, context, emotional expression, relationships, and power. A great source for this information is http://www. culturaldetective.com.

67

- Understand the difference between stereotypes and cultural generalizations. There is a danger that when people begin to learn about difference they will begin to stereotype people based on their culture. Cultural generalizations—the way groups have shared customs, values, and ways of organizing the world—are real, but they are neutral descriptors used to help expand and point out the complexity of identity, whereas stereotypes are judgments that simplify and overgeneralize.

- In the example above, the real question to ask is whether Sandra's way of being is a problem of effectiveness or just a problem of preference for John. If it is a problem of effectiveness, Sandra can be instructed about ways to improve without being insulted. Cultural norms can be adjusted—after all, becoming mutually adaptive means movement from both sides. Just because Sandra may feel more comfortable being one way doesn't mean she can't make adjustments. If, on the other hand, it is John's judgment that is personal and clouded, then Sandra should talk about John's behavior with a more senior person whom she trusts, perhaps a mentor or someone the force has designated to support diversity.

- Sandra could also try to find out whether other officers are having a problem with her communication or have had a difficult time working with her. If so, Sandra could ask for any suggestions they might have about how she could make improvements to her delivery without fundamentally changing how she expresses herself. What Sandra should not do is keep it to herself. It is particularly important that Sandra have a chance to put John's behavior in context and solve the problem, which could include finding someone else to work with who appreciates her capabilities and embraces difference.

- Each organization can look closely at its values and cultural norms—those that are articulated as well as those that are unwritten. Do those values and ways of doing things make space for difference to be respected and developed so that the organization and the individuals in it thrive? Or are people judged by a narrow set of preferences where there is only one right and superior way? After answering these questions, an organization is ready to make changes to its policies and practices to ensure talented people develop and find different ways to contribute to the organization's mission and purpose.

HABIT #15: DON'T MISTAKE
THE MIRROR FOR MERIT
AVOID IN-GROUP FAVORITISM

I used to think that I was a great interviewer—ethical, fair, and open—until one day, while working as a young lawyer, I was asked to interview two individuals from top-ranked law schools for a new associate position. One was an African-American female who had received her undergraduate degree from a Seven Sisters college (like me) and had competed in intercollegiate sports during her time there (like me). The other was a white man (unlike me) whose resume indicated he had served in the military (unlike me), and was the captain of the golf team (I have never played golf) in college. Can you guess which interview was animated and which one lackluster?

Culturally Ineffective: Mistaking the Mirror for Merit

The first interviewee was a black woman; I am a black woman. She played softball; I was the center for my college basketball team. She attended Wellesley; I went to Barnard. Are you getting the picture? I assessed her based on my own attributes. In fact, I acted as if the interview were really only a formality—what I really wanted to say was "Why don't we just go for a drink?" In diversity work we call this in-group favoritism. In-group favoritism is not a prejudice *against* a group as much as it is about favoring others who are part of your group.

Only when both of my interviewees left, did it dawn on me: I had been unfair to each candidate. My biases had totally directed both my questions and how I sorted and valued the answers. Basically I had only been interested in looking in the mirror and seeing my own reflection, and my behavior had influenced the quality of both the interviews and the candidates' experiences in the interviews.

In-group favoritism points to a particular challenge of being culturally effective: the pitfall that many of us are more interested in replicating ourselves than in growing diversity. You may not even realize that you are making positive assumptions about the person you are evaluating because of the positive associations you have toward a neighborhood, school, background, or company—the neighborhood, school, background, or company that you trust and with which are comfortable. On the other hand, the person you interview whose experiences don't resonate with you may be quite qualified, but you may not be able to see it because you are put off by their apparent differences.

In the workplaces where I consult, I also see in-group favoritism playing a major role in deciding who will receive the stretch assignment, who will be the point person for the highest-profile or riskiest opportunities, or who will be elected to the top positions. While merit is an important aspect of the decision, the final choice is often based on subjective qualities like fit or the decision-maker's gut. Unfortunately, gut and fit are highly influenced by "likeness." To like yourself is a good thing, but you can't have diversity and all of its benefits if your organization is only duplicating the dominant culture through its practices and policies—something we call organizational preference. Unbeknownst to the company's leaders, this organizational preference may be standing in the way of the organization's excellence.

Tips for Practicing This Culturally Effective Habit: Avoid In-Group Favoritism

- Try not to look for only people who are like you when you are selecting individuals for opportunities
- Look around you; are you surrounded by "mini-me's"? Identify competencies, communication, learning styles, perspectives, and experiences that you don't

have but could enhance your life, team, organization, or community. Begin in earnest to hire, advance, and include people who possess such capabilities.

- If you are selecting someone from a group of people for an opportunity, remember to consider the whole list of possible candidates from whom you could choose. If you choose from your mental list, you will often miss someone who is capable but different from you.

- If you are a leader, rotate opportunities and resources so that you can check the in-group favoritism that may be unintentionally enabling only certain people to succeed while making others feel excluded and demotivated.

- If you are in an interview situation like I was, notice not only when a feeling of discomfort arises, but also when one of unwarranted ease arises—these are clues that you may be prone to bias against or for another individual.

- Dig a little more deeply into the candidate's experiences, especially if you don't share them. Regarding the second interviewee in my story above, what if I had acknowledged my lack of familiarity with the military and asked him about his motivation, his ability to deal with difficult situations, and his leadership skills?

- Don't make assumptions about the interviewee—where he grew up, what he has experienced, what he likes and doesn't like. These assumptions are usually stereotypes about groups, and if you lead with questions that are rooted in stereotypes, you may offend the candidate and lose the opportunity to bring a talented person into your organization. (As an example, white male interviewer to a South Asian woman: "Are you sure your Indian parents are going to let you come to New York to work alone?" To a black male candidate: "One of the best things about us is that we have a great basketball team.")

- If you don't know about entries on a resume (associations, articles, group

73

memberships), don't ignore those things because they are unfamiliar to you; inquire about them. These questions may lead to some of the most valuable insights about what makes a candidate unique, and whether or not he or she is right for the position.

- If you are interviewing for an organization that has made a commitment to diversity, make sure you share information about your diversity commitment and policies with every candidate, not only those from underrepresented groups. You can't tell what people are interested in or have a sensitivity to or affinity with, so don't make assumptions. After all, your diversity program is about making the entire organization better, so everyone should hear about and plan to be a part of moving these values forward.

- Take your cue from interviewees. If they bring up concerns about gender issues or speak about humble backgrounds, this is a signal that you could engage a conversation around these subjects. But even then, be careful to seek information rather than assuming. Also, during the conversation you may realize that the candidate could benefit from speaking to someone else in your organization who shares a certain identity or life experience. It is great to offer a promising candidate the opportunity to meet such a person.

HABIT #16: AREN'T YOU SCARED TO LIVE THERE?
IF YOU SEE SOMETHING, SAY SOMETHING

A small group of white managers and their supervisees, including Roberto, a new Mexican-American employee who has recently moved to the city, are talking together at a cocktail reception preceding an important company-wide dinner. Roberto is the first Latino in this particular division of the organization. One of the managers in the group asks him where he has decided to live. When Roberto answers with the name of a mostly Spanish-speaking urban neighborhood, the manager remarks, "Really? Aren't you scared to live there?" The circle grows a little quiet, and Roberto responds by talking about how much he appreciates his short commute to the office.

Culturally Ineffective: Being a Passive Bystander—"Excuse Me, I Think I Need Another Drink"
Often, in a situation like this, other people in the cluster feel the same way as the manager who spoke up, but there are also people who are utterly horrified that this manager is about to reverse all the work that the diversity committee has done in the last year to increase the diversity among their employees. Most of the time, in a scenario like this, someone will try to change the subject, or folks will find a convenient excuse to walk away. In this case, Roberto recalled that he felt upset, but since he had just come to this company and didn't want to be unpleasant or overreact, he tried to remain gracious, saying, "The commute works really well for my family and me."

What is required from those who want to be culturally effective is something we in the business call interrupting bias or being an active bystander: using various techniques to speak up, point out, and help defuse a potentially offensive situation or unacceptable behavior. When bystanders intervene in a situation like the one above, there are many beneficial results. The person offended can see that he has allies in the organization—he may be underrepresented as a one-down group member, but he is not alone. The diversity commitment of the organization is made more real and further unacceptable behavior is discouraged. This active stance also encourages more respectful behavior and provides a model for what can be done when the organization's norms and values are violated. Interrupting bias helps to create more of a community of accountability and increases morale. This inclusive and respectful community, in turn, makes it more possible to attract and retain a diverse workforce that works together effectively. But how is it done?

Between coming on like a house on fire and standing around awkwardly wishing you were somewhere (anywhere!) else, there are some useful—and graceful— approaches to handling an unfortunate scene like this one that will lead everyone present toward greater understanding and better behavior. Finding the courage as a bystander to say something is one step; figuring out what you want to say is the other half of the battle. Of course, if the behavior is egregious, intentional, or physically threatening, intervening, no matter what you say, is better than saying nothing. However, sometimes the infraction is a micro-inequity as described in Habit #12, "She Was So Articulate." Many people find it harder to intervene when the offense is more subtle, when they know that the person responsible is well-meaning or his or her behavior is unconscious and unintentional.

Interrupting bias is a skill that works well when a member of the in-group or one-up group—someone on the more privileged side of the chart—does the interrupting. So the white people or even someone in the crowd who has a one-up position because of job status (for example, another manager) could be effective in interrupting in this situation. When someone from the more privileged status interrupts, it works be-

76

cause that person is usually not regarded as too sensitive or having a personal axe to grind. The intervention also may carry more authority by virtue of the interrupter's privileged status. The comments may be easier for the offender to hear because they are coming from a person who is perceived as a member of the same one-up group.

I know that it may feel really difficult to say something in meetings or in a group when you witness biased behavior. You have many relationships to worry about, and your personality may make it difficult to speak up in a group in general. Also, you may be so confused or hurt by the behavior, even when it occurs in a one-on-one situation, that you don't know what to say. Studies on being an active bystander suggest that there are many reasons why people don't interrupt bad behavior, but when individuals can overcome those reasons and interject in real time, it works best. But let's face it—many of us are not always going to be able to find the right tone or comment to interrupt the behavior in the moment, especially if we are concerned about embarrassing the offender or if there is a power differential between us and the offending party. In a situation like the one above, you can always go back and bring the subject up with the person or group responsible for the behavior when you have your wits about you, have cooled off, and have thought of a constructive way to approach the issue.

Bottom line, it's hard to be culturally effective in this area and know how to respond in the moment or later unless you practice doing so. Also, the more you practice all the Habits in this book, the more you will gain the confidence that you can make a difference when an unforeseen situation arises.

Tips for Practicing This Culturally Effective Habit: If You See Something Say Something

- Be an active bystander. When you decide to say something in a scenario like the one above, use a tone of voice that is welcoming and nonjudgmental, perhaps infused by humor or a light touch: You might say, "Don't worry, we have diversity training coming up this fall, right, X?" (Say this with a friendly tone, a smile, and maybe a comforting hand on the manager's back). The important thing is treat the offending person with respect—recognize that this may be a sign that they need attention or may be upset. If you speak from your heart, what you say will naturally carry the power and credibility to open the hearts and minds of others.

- Remember that when you do interrupt bias you should do so with an "I" statement, such as "I have a hard time hearing...." or "I'm feeling pain for the *so-and-so* people...." You might choose to be a little daring and make a comment such as "I don't think we use that word anymore" or simply "Ouch!"

- One woman in a workshop I facilitated recently gave me another great statement: "I don't think I am the right audience for that comment (or this e-mail)." She explained that she finds it quite useful at family events with relatives who are speaking in stereotypes about a one-down group, or on social media and e-mail where people are forwarding certain distasteful or hateful jokes, cartoons, or articles. I love it. It definitely puts an end to the behavior in the moment.

- You might choose to ask a question, such as "Why do you say that?" or "What do you mean by that?" You might offer a different point of view, such as "Actually, my experience has been...." Maybe as someone in this awkward cocktail-party circle, you could say to the Latino employee, "I'm sure he doesn't know that he just insulted you." You could ask the manager about the meaning of the comment. In other words, don't presume. Sometimes when you ask what a person meant, you discover that they really didn't mean what you thought; their foundation is good, but they were just awkward or less than artful in expressing an idea. Or sometimes the person is actually saying something you know not to say, but if the truth be told, you have the same feeling or question. You can say things such as, "X, what are you asking? I am sure that Roberto wouldn't have moved there if he felt unsafe." Or you might ask in a curious, rather than accusatory tone, "X, have you ever spent any time there?"

- Or perhaps you could be bold and say, "You know, I have to admit, I haven't spent much time in that part of town. You know how some of us white folks can be; we rarely venture outside of our own neighborhoods. Can you tell us more about the community? What attracted you to it?"

- You might want to practice first interrupting friends or family or in low-risk situations when bias statements are made. Remember, success leaves clues and keeps you aware and able to do more interrupting on the spot.

HABIT #17: "I KNOW YOU HAVEN'T DONE THIS BEFORE"
DON'T BE AFRAID TO ASK

I was recently in a crowded train station with folks scurrying to get replacement tickets because their trains had been canceled. While standing in a long line, I noticed a blind guy standing alongside the line who seemed very agitated. I asked if he needed something, and he told me that he was trying to make a train that was boarding. I knew enough to ask if he wanted me to help him to the platform; he replied that he would, so I took his hand and started to lead him. In a polite but firm way, however, he took my hand away and put his hand on my shoulder. I adjusted quickly and began to lead him quickly. Unfortunately, I led him into (yes, I mean literally into) two columns. Each time that I heard his shoulder hit the pole, I said, "I'm so sorry; am I supposed to be calling these things out?" He said, "Yes, but it's okay, I know you've never done this before." By the time I got him to the track, there were stairs, and I called them out. I said, "We're here, mind the gap." He thanked me and boarded. So much learned in so little time!

Culturally Ineffective: Not Asking and Assuming You Know What You Don't Know

We often assume that we know how best to assist someone in a situation like the one above and we are off to the races without ever asking the individual what he or she would prefer. If we haven't spent time with people with disabilities, for example, it is quite likely we in the one-up group will get it wrong because it is not necessary for us to learn about those in the one-down group. As a result, we sometimes act in ways that ignore their wishes and treat them as helpless and dependent. We don't need to beat ourselves up about it, but we do need to ask and learn what to do to create inclusion for groups that have been traditionally excluded. This usually requires us to learn new things or to broaden our awareness of the barriers to access we are creating. This especially is true when it comes to disability, given that many of us lack exposure to persons with disabilities.

For example, an associate of mine, Perry, reported a situation that occurred in his writing class. He had prepared a series of diagrams for the first class but was thrown off track when he noticed that one of his students was blind. Perry hurried through the materials. The student, realizing that Perry did not know what to do, said to him, "It's really okay. Just explain what it is the rest of the class is looking at, and I'll be able to follow too." Perry did so, and in the follow-up exercise the student, using his speech-to-text computer, created a fabulous spreadsheet that became the talk of the class the following week. He might not have been able to look at the class examples, but he could certainly see the point of what was going on!

People often freeze when they encounter situations like Perry's or mine in the train station. Common sense gets derailed because we are afraid that we will offend a person with a disability by asking if he or she needs our assistance. So, we often remain silent when we see a blind person heading toward an obstacle; yet we call out to warn a sighted person of an upcoming obstacle of which he or she is unaware. We see the disability rather than the person and forget to treat a person with a disability just as we want to be treated. As a result, we avoid individuals who have disabilities and miss out on their participation and capabilities.

Tips for Practicing This Culturally Effective Habit: Don't Be Afraid to Ask

- Don't be freaked out or freeze when you encounter a person who appears to be different from you. Don't worry about the mistakes you might make in an interaction. Use common sense; don't abandon it.

- However, just because you are a good, well-meaning person doesn't mean that you know how to be respectful of difference in every situation. You have to learn what you don't know. Don't assume you know based on your position of advantage. That position has created a lack of awareness of and discomfort with certain differences. When I was attempting to guide the blind man in the train station, I didn't know to call out the upcoming columns and their location, resulting in him running directly into them.
- Ask before you act. Ask the person if he or she needs assistance and, if so, how. Things would have gone much smoother had I only asked the blind passenger in the train station to tell me what to do because I had never done this before.
- Plan ahead if you are in Perry's position so you don't exclude a person with a disability from fully and equally participating and contributing, or make them feel stuck or embarrassed. Ask participants ahead of time if they have any special needs. Provide a contact name with a telephone number and an e-mail address on any registration forms. Inform any speakers ahead of time of those special needs so that they can ensure that their presentations are accessible. If there are handouts, make them available in an electronic format. If videos are used, make sure that it is captioned. When you make accessibility a priority in the planning stages, you create a welcoming and inclusive environment, as we mention in Habit #10, "Real Inclusion Is in the Details."
- Incorporating universal design into your presentations, workshops, or meetings will benefit even persons who don't have disabilities. People learn in different ways; some are more visual, some are more auditory, and some learn more through movement and interaction. In Perry's case, his blind student's

spreadsheet benefited the entire class.

- Persons with the same disability aren't the same. Don't assume that what worked for one will work for another. No group is a monolith, and individuals from the same group will have different needs, reactions, responses, and ways of handling situations.
- Finally, treat people with disabilities the way you would want to be treated.
- For more specific ways to make your meetings and events inclusive of those with disabilities, check out this informative "Planning Accessible Meeting and Events" tool kit created by the American Bar Association's Commission on Disability Rights at http://www.americanbar.org/groups/disabilityrights.html.

HABIT #18: GIRL, I MEAN, BOY, I MEAN, YOU KNOW....
USE YOUR MISTAKES TO GROW

I was asked by a firm to do a training for their employees on LGBT (lesbian/gay/bisexual/transgender) issues. I chose to work with a colleague who is a transgender male, Tony. The last time I had seen Tony, he was Toni, female and presenting and identified as a lesbian. I still remember the first time we met after he was transitioning. I was on vacation, and one night I ran into him at a restaurant club on the dance floor. He was with a mutual friend, Karen, whom I recognized. I was talking to Karen and acknowledged Tony with a smile, the way you do when you meet someone you don't know who is with someone you do. Then Tony took my arm, turned me around to face him and said, "Vernā , it's Toni; except now I'm Tony." I looked closer and said, "Toni?! Wow, you look amazing. I didn't recognize you. You look so good. Look at your shirt, your muscles. Unbelievable! How are you?!" I was shocked and didn't try to play it off, but I was also enthusiastic and supportive. He wrote me an e-mail later and said that my reaction was the best he had received and made him feel great. So a year later I reached out to Tony, to do a training with me. We planned the training and I remember being very conscious of making sure that I was using the accurate pronoun with Tony and not saying things like "Girl, you know..." and "Girl, why don't you…" But when I got on my feet in front of lots of people in the training, I said, referring to Tony, "I want to reiterate what she mentioned…" or "Her example shows…."

Culturally Ineffective: Shying Away from Mistakes
When Tony quietly pointed out to me during the break that I had referred to him as *her*, I was surprised. "I did?" "Yes, several times," he said, "and when you wrote my

name you wrote it as *Toni*," (which, of course, is how he had spelled his name when he was female identified). I apologized, scolded myself, and committed to getting it right for the rest of the training. Then I started talking and kept making the mistake, so I decided to just use it as a learning moment—I shared it with participants. I apologized to Tony publicly and I asked him and the audience to point it out when I made a mistake. I made many mistakes that day and afterward, but I made fewer as the time went on. Tony was amazingly patient. He explained that I had known him first as a woman so it was harder for me to break that association and that over time as I got to know him as a man, it wouldn't be as hard. Because I decided to put the learning process front and center, the attendees got to see what happens when you don't shy away from mistakes: you learn…slowly but surely; we all do. We evolve, especially when we have someone as forgiving and capable as Tony to help us along.

Tips for Practicing This Culturally Effective Habit: Use Your Mistakes to Grow

- Adopt a humble attitude toward what we call cultural competence, the ability to interact effectively with people of different backgrounds, identities, and cultures. There is no perfection in this game. If you are a perfectionist, this work is not for you. You have to make peace with the idea that you were raised in a culture where you were taught implicitly or explicitly that some groups were better than others. We all were! When you think a group or culture is inferior, immoral, untrustworthy, and so forth, you don't learn about it, and you don't spend time trying to interact or be conversant with that group. There is much to unlearn and much misinformation and lack of information we have to overcome. Since we all have some catching up to do, there is no room for blame or shame.

- Learn how much you don't know and the reasons you don't know. When I took the step of revealing in our training session what I didn't know, where I personally was stuck, I could feel the entire room relax. At that point we all had the opportunity to evolve.

- Don't make the one-down person do all the work of teaching you how to treat them in culturally respectful way—we can't expect that transgender people will all be as patient as Tony. Take it upon yourself to learn more by reading about cultures and differences that you are not familiar with, especially if you know that you are going to be talking to or working with people from that background. Take the time to learn the right terms and language. As a cisgendered person (the term for people whose gender identity or gender role assigned to it by society matches with the sex they were assigned at birth), it never occurred to me that people could feel differently. I took my reality about gender and gender identity as the way it is for everyone. Transgender individuals may be the most misunderstood one-down group in our society today. There are more resources for individuals and companies regarding transgender people than there used to be. Check out GLAAD's Transgender Resources at http://www.glaad.org/transgender and the resources listed on this Oberlin University site: http://new.oberlin.edu/office/multicultural-resource-center/workshops/trans-101.dot.

- As a rule of thumb, try not to flood a person with questions once you find out they are transgender, even though you might be naturally curious. This is a good rule whenever you approach someone who is significantly different from you, especially if the questions go to their one-down identity. If you feel the transgender person would welcome some questions, try to stick to the questions that you would ask someone who is not transgender. For example, you

87

don't normally ask people you don't know about their body, so don't ask these questions of a transgender person you just met. You could ask what pronoun they prefer, where they grew up, what they do for work, questions like that. Some transgender people might enjoy the role of educator, but most people don't want to engage in deep personal questions before there is any kind of trust or relationship has been developed. These are just common-sense guidelines to apply as you begin. Obviously there is heterogeneity in every group, so expect difference and stay open and aware of the individual with whom you are interacting.

- You can also consult people who are like you but have done work to be more culturally competent with the culture or background with which you are trying to understand or work more effectively and inclusively.

- Welcome correction as an opportunity for learning and for deepening relationships. Change is hard even when you are committed to that change—and changing one's language can be especially difficult. But the experience can be invaluable even as it makes you more aware of your shortcomings.

- Get accustomed to making mistakes. It is inevitable once you operate outside of your comfort zone! It's a good sign, actually. You can't possibly know everything about every group or culture, but you can work on knowing more and on getting better. The most important thing is adopting the attitude that cultural competence is an important skill to have and you will do what it takes, including risking embarrassment, to keep moving forward.

- Engage, rather than disengage. I have to admit that I thought that one way to end the torture for both Tony and me was to withdraw from the relationship. But I was grateful for his grace and knew it would be wrong to respond by avoiding him.

HABIT #19: LOVE IS HAVING TO SAY YOU'RE SORRY
LEARN TO APOLOGIZE

A friend I know who is hard at work on diversity issues told me that she was attending a vocal music recital with a parent who has a daughter adopted from Asia. But when she asked about the daughter, she called her by the name of the other Asian-American girl in the chorus (who had also been adopted). My friend noticed that for a brief moment the father of the girl she had meant to identify looked confused, but then continued on with the conversation. After the incident, my friend realized what she had done wrong. She fretted about it all day. I can imagine how I would feel in such a situation, wishing that I had never opened my mouth or hoping that maybe he hadn't heard me. My friend told her husband about what she had done at the concert. He consoled her and told her it wasn't a big deal, and, besides, what could she do anyway? Surely this father got that kind of mix-up all the time.

Culturally Ineffective: "It Was a Natural Mistake; Dwelling on It Only Makes It Worse"

When we make a mistake with people we care about and see we have hurt them, our healthy urge is to apologize. The reason we apologize is that we realize our intent was not the same as our impact. Or we realize that even though what we intended to say or do may have been valid and important, it wasn't the whole equation. We want the relationship to continue to breathe and grow, so we apologize.

However, when we move out of our intimate circle and our behavior upsets someone, sometimes our natural instinct is to defend ourselves by sharing our intent instead of accepting responsibility for our impact. We say things like "That's not what I meant," or "I didn't mean to insult you." Most people in a one-down group can accept this kind of explanation if you apologize first and acknowledge how the action or comment might have been offensive.

In this case, the father at the chorus concert may not have been from a one-down group, but having an adopted daughter has more than likely exposed him to his share of staring, misunderstanding, and assumptions, which are frustrating at best and wounding to both him and his child at worst.

Because my friend is hard at work on racial issues she took a very courageous step. She sat with her feelings for a few more hours and then she picked up the phone. She called the father and apologized for calling his daughter by the other Asian girl's name. The father listened, thanked her for calling, and assured her that everything was fine. They talked a little about how their girls both enjoyed music and what options were available in the town outside of the school program. The father went on to explain that his daughter had been adopted from the same part of Korea as the other girl in the chorus—both families had even gone through the same social services agency.

Maybe the mistake wasn't a big deal, but the call and the apology certainly were. It so rarely happens that someone is willing to admit to a mistake when they are not called on it, especially across race. I can only imagine the possibilities for a real relationship between all of these girls in the chorus, because one parent was courageous enough to say, "I made a mistake that may have been a little culturally ineffective, and I want to account for it."

One thing that I have seen in the workplace is that people are afraid that apologizing will get them in more trouble—that it will be used against them as an admission of guilt. However, I find that when people don't apologize for the small things and then the person whom they slighted is passed up for an opportunity or receives a bad review, the slighted person has a reason to assume that the offending party is insensitive and perhaps acting on racial animus orbias.

People know that no one is perfect; what they don't like is when we pretend to be. I think they are just looking for some acknowledgement that we understand our mistake and are more committed to being culturally effective than preserving our self-image as a good person. When we downplay or ignore the mistake, we often exacerbate the situation or make it impossible to develop an authentic and trusting relationship with the person and perhaps his or her community of colleagues and friends.

Tips for Practicing This Culturally Effective Habit: Learn to Apologize

- Apologizing is not a sign of weakness. Matter-of-fact apologetic comments actually demonstrate a great deal of personal power and high self-regard. If the individual you have insulted does not forgive you, or insists on buffeting your apology in an attempt to extract more or embarrass you, that has more to do with them. If you apologize sincerely, you have done your job.
- Don't be stingy or begrudging with your apology; people can tell and it will not be well-received.
- Don't go way over the top with your apology, either, which makes people uncomfortable. It may be regarded as disingenuous.
- Identify that you are apologizing. Different cultures have different ways of coming clean; some may depend heavily on context, while others rely more on humor. An apology should look and feel like an apology—give it the attention it deserves.
- Apologizing is always easier and cleaner when it comes earlier on in a situa-

tion. Here some words you might start with in a variety of situations that call for an apology:

» "I'm sorry; I see that I offended you. What did I say to upset you?" or "I wish I knew, but I don't and I want to know."

» "What should I have said?"

» "Did I just call you the name of the other (Latina, lesbian, etc.)? Sorry. Bear with me; I'm working on it."

» "That was wrong, wasn't it?"

» "Oh, shoot, that was sexist, wasn't it?"

Or if you happen to be like one of my male friends who confided he has been taught as a man to "apologize for nothing," especially in the workplace, you might try the "guy" version of these statements. It goes something like this: "Just ignore (kill, shoot, etc.) me. I'm an idiot (jerk, fool, Neanderthal, insensitive clod)!"

- Sometimes people from one-down groups have been injured so many times that your comment or behavior is the last straw and your apology will not be enough to mend the impact of the *isms* they have been encountering through-out their lifetime. They are exhausted often and distrustful of anyone from the one-up group. All you can do is commit to helping to dismantle the *isms* by working on your cultural competence to avoid mistakes where possible and using your advantages to make a difference.

HABIT #20: HAVE COFFEE (OR TEA)
EXPAND YOUR COMFORT ZONE AND PROFESSIONAL AND SOCIAL CIRCLES

Joan was on the board of a synagogue that was planning an interfaith weekend with a local black church to celebrate Martin Luther King, Jr. Day. Joan's fellow board members were enthused about "doing the right thing" and conducted spirited pre-planning discussions with their partner-church members about all of the activities that were going to take place. The problem was that every one of these pre-planning meetings was held either at the synagogue (whose members were almost entirely white), or at one of the synagogue board member's houses (all the members were white) a good distance from the church. When Joan suggested to her board that they travel to the black church for some of the meetings, or gather in a great cafe she knew that was located in the church's neighborhood, the other members looked at her, stunned. Their instinct—even when planning a diversity event—had been to stay on their home turf and within their comfort zone. It didn't occur to them, for example, that some people from the church had to take public transportation to travel to and from the meetings. Once they realized this, several assented to Joan's idea. One board member even told Joan later that he was surprised at himself: he truly expected that he could have the feeling of doing good without putting anything on the line personally.

Culturally Ineffective: "That's Why They Call It a Comfort Zone"

There's a reason they call it a comfort zone—because remaining within a bounded and familiar set of experiences can be very relaxing. The smells, sounds, behaviors, verbiage, dress, and expectations are all familiar, and familiar can feel nice. However, if you want to be culturally effective, you have to be willing to expand your social circle, engage new networks, and get outside of your comfort zone. You definitely have to learn to go to places where people of all backgrounds will feel comfortable. You also have to be willing to go places where you might not feel comfortable so that you can get to know and interact with people unlike you. If you want to know how to say the right thing or how not to say the wrong thing, you have to connect.

Why is this important for culturally effective people? One, you learn more about other cultures by being around them, not by being around yourself. Two, if you are a person with some influence and power, you will be able to lend that influence to those talented people in your company and community from the one-down group who can take advantage your connections to succeed and excel or just to feel welcomed and at home. What it means for you is that you get to be exposed to new things, develop more comfort with difference, break down the barriers to inclusion for all, and take advantage of the richness of diversity.

Expanding to new networks and relationships ultimately causes self-examination and, hopefully, personal growth. The members of the synagogue made the same mistake many of us do when we attempt to create new networks and work together across differences—they operated unknowingly from a position of power and privilege. We are kind and well-meaning people, but we are still operating inside the chart we explored in Habit #1, "Understand the *isms*." We baby boomers, for example, say we want to understand and work with millennials in our organization, but we quickly revert to adultism, bossing them around and assuming we know best. Then we wonder why these young people don't seem as engaged in our organization and leave so quickly.

Actually, in the scenario we started with, both groups know what it means to be one-down—the synagogue with regard to religion and the church with regard to race and for some parishioners, social economic status. They are also both situated on the one-up column of our chart as Protestants (the church) and white and, in some cases, middle and upper class (the synagogue). When groups like these make the concerted effort to engage and traverse the columns on the chart, and are able to suspend their stereotypes and tolerate temporary discomfort, they are disrupting the *isms*. When the intentional connection is done with respect and humility, it allows individuals to appreciate, question, and change the structures that exclude and disadvantage both groups.

Tips for Practicing This Culturally Effective Habit: Expand Your Comfort Zone and Social and Professional Circles

- Diversify the group of individuals with whom you socialize, instead of going out with the same people all the time. Start off slowly with the expansion; you don't have to take on a big project across town. You can just invite for coffee someone whom you wouldn't ask normally. Personally, I prefer tea. It could be someone at your workplace, sports club, committee, school, or board. You don't have to go into the interaction planning to talk about deep subjects. Even newspaper topics such as sports or travel are a beginning. It can then lead to a deeper sharing about an individual's hobbies, background, and history, if approached in the right spirit.
- You can progress to lunch, dinner, or drinks. It's great to invite folks to your home for dinner, but just like our synagogue friends, don't only welcome them to your house—visit them in their homes, neighborhoods, and hangouts.
- When you seek to find out what someone is doing in their life, and what they care about, remember to also share your life; tell them the things that you truly care about. Sometimes just connecting with someone on a personal level

does as much good as any intentional diversity effort or activity we might undertake.

- When you expand your circle at work and you are together socially, go beyond superficial discussions. Any subject matter can be developed into a personal encounter: if you are talking about work, don't just ask about what someone is doing, ask who they are doing it with, what excites them about a project, how they are managing the chief obstacles, and where a certain project might take them in terms of added skills and further opportunities. By the way, people are dying to talk to someone more senior about their future and dreams. So if you happen to be a supervisor, manager, or senior person in the organization, you have much to offer.

- Speaking of being senior, think of people you have mentored over the years—do you see any patterns? Have you contributed to the success of only those who are most like you, or do your past mentoring relationships include those who are quite different? You may not be intending to send a message of exclusion, but mentoring people like you in your circle of comfort communicates that you are not interested in developing diversified relationships, especially if you are a manager or leader of a group or organization. Some people erroneously think they can't mentor a person who is different from them with regard to some significant dimension of identity. Many of the women who are now at the top of their organizations were mentored by men because at the time they were coming up, there were no women to mentor them. Reflect on how you can develop a more diverse set of mentoring relationships.

- When planning or sponsoring events and locations for your organization or team or with another individual, make sure you are considering the interests and comfort of others, not just your own or those of the majority. Many times people from one-down groups are accused of not being good team players or being antisocial. But some women (not all) don't want to go golfing or hunting; many LGBT folks may be concerned about their safety in certain parts of the city; the location may not be handicap accessible; that club might have a history of excluding people of color; some people due to religious convictions may not wish to be at events that center on drinking. You may say, "Well, how am I supposed to know all of that?" or "That's a lot of accommodating!" It's not as hard as you think. Pull together a diverse group to plan events in your organization, and when socializing with an individual or a team, ask where they like to go. If you don't ask, some people will go along to get along, but won't enjoy themselves. In some cases they may be offended by the activity or event. Some people politely say, "No, thank you," and you have no idea that what they are really saying is "Are you kidding? That's the last place I want to go to have fun."

97

- One of the most exciting ways you can increase your cultural effectiveness is to seek out opportunities where you can make yourself a minority. You can increase your exposure to different cultures by attending unfamiliar religious centers, book talks with writers from other backgrounds, or events with musicians where you will not be in the majority. Putting yourself in these places may seem scary at first. Almost all of the time, however, when you reach out to the other people you encounter in these situations, they will be excited to share their practices, ideas, and creations with you. For the most part, these are individuals who will welcome you because they know what it's like to feel unwelcome. Having been in your position, they know and practice what worked to make them feel more comfortable.

- One warning: don't go barreling in with your superiority blazing when practicing this habit. I know, you wouldn't do it consciously, but sometimes, in our one-up identities, we are unaware of how much space we take up and how much attention we demand. We are offensive and condescending and we don't know it. Be aware of how you enter the conversations and places described above. Be a listener and a collaborator. Don't try to be the "knower" or to master the situation—it won't go well.

HABIT #21: BEING PROACTIVE DOESN'T MEAN TAKING A SECOND JOB
COMMIT MICRO-AFFIRMATIONS

One junior Latino associate in a large accounting firm told me that it made a world of difference when a managing director invited him out to a sporting event when they were both attending an out-of-town conference. The director discussed high-level practice development during their pre-event dinner and then allowed for some more relaxed dialogue during the game. But the associate said the part of the night that lingered the most was the director's offhand comment: "I hope you're still here in five years; we need people of your caliber to get where we want to go." It wasn't so much the "wining and dining" as much as the sincerity of the compliment and the director's view of him as a contributor to the firm's future success that made the associate think more seriously about committing to a future with the firm.

Culturally Ineffective: "I Don't Have Time to Be Inclusive"
Some people, especially in the workplace, explain to me that they don't have time to be inclusive. They have too much work to do. What I hear from members of under-represented groups who have been historically excluded from the power structure of these organizations is that the smallest things make them feel more or less included, more or less respected, and more or less valued and visible in their organizations, schools, and communities. It is not that these individuals aren't going to make their own efforts to integrate and engage, it is just much easier, quicker, and more comfortable when those who are in the majority meet them halfway.

If you are a person who is better represented in an organization or better reflected in the culture in a particular environment, you have the power to make the road of belonging smoother. If you are among the leadership of the organization, you have even more opportunity to use small but meaningful gestures that signal acceptance and respect. We spoke about micro-insults in Habit #2, "I Hope She Can Drive"—small slights that accumulate to make people feel excluded. Well, micro-affirmations, small acts of kindness and inclusion, can just as easily make a positive difference for people.

Tips for Practicing This Culturally Effective Habit: Commit Micro-Affirmations

- Instead of keeping silent or withdrawing from others whom you perceive as different because you are afraid of committing a micro-inequity, decide to commit to doing small things that affirm respect and inclusion. You can speak to people in the one-down groups in places where they are underrepresented. Acknowledge them (don't stare!) at the grocery store, at the school concert, at the PTO meeting, on the soccer field, in the elevator, at a reception, in the lobby, on your floor, or when you see them sitting by themselves on the bleachers. You don't have to make a big deal of it; just make contact.
- Make sure to introduce people who are with you to those around you in the office. Don't ignore some and pay attention to others.
- Drop by someone's office and shoot the breeze. Engage in a conversation in the break room. You would be surprised how the smallest contact can make a person feel seen and appreciated.
- Pay attention to people you generally include in telephone calls, meetings, e-mails, and communications. Who are you missing? Oversights are easy to fix, once you see them. If there is a reason you have excluded someone, that might be a larger conversation or intervention. But I encourage you not to ignore the

issue. It is hard for people to contribute or perform at their highest potential if they don't have the information they need or they feel excluded. Exclusion worsens performance.

- Remember to say thank you and to acknowledge individual contributions. Tell people specifically about what you like about their work or behavior. Many times people are doing well, but they don't know it, because, in many workplaces, praise is not part of the culture.

- When talking to people, give them your attention rather than staring at your mobile devices or computer screens. Don't take calls in the middle of conversations unless you absolutely have to. If you are expecting a call, let the person know beforehand.

- Make it a point to know the people on your team and what they care about. Be able to ask them appropriate questions about their hobbies, their families, their vacations. These are signs that you care enough to notice.

- Try to make schedules with other people's obligations in mind, not only your own. This is extremely important for people working flex-time or part-time schedules, for people who are religiously observant, or for people working in other time zones. Think about what time you hold most meetings or events. Does it regularly exclude some people? Can you can change or alternate the times?

- Learn to share the credit for team efforts. Tell others about the contributions and successes that individuals have had. This is especially important for one-down group members because bias and stereotype may be preventing people from fully appreciating their accomplishments.

HABIT #22: DON'T BE A
SLOPPY SENTIMENTALIST
KEEP YOUR STANDARDS HIGH

Jessica, a white woman, is a mentor for Evangeline, a young African-American woman who is one of a select group of fellows in a STEM (Science, Technology, Engineering, and Mathematics) training program at Jessica's technology company. The program is part of a pipeline project to attract more women and people of color to STEM professions and the company. Jessica really likes Evangeline and wants her to excel in the program, but she has just heard from a colleague who worked with Evangeline on her last assignment that her work was late and was missing several sections.

This is not the first time Jessica has heard an unsatisfactory report about Evangeline. Early on in the yearlong program, Evangeline's first assignment didn't go very well, but Jessica had ignored the supervisor's comment since he was known to be a harsh critic. In addition, he had made several offensive remarks about how the company shouldn't be running a "social welfare program." When Jessica reflected, she remembered she had been the one who had advocated that Evangeline be included in the program even though some on the training program selection committee didn't think her candidacy was strong enough. Jessica had been impressed with how bright and determined Evangeline was and she knew how important the job would be to Evangeline and her family. Evangeline was the first in her family to go to college and she had shared with Jessica how much she wanted to be able to help her younger sister pay for her education.

It is now six months into the program, and if Evangeline doesn't start doing better, she will not move on from the training program to a permanent position with the company. Jessica has not discussed any of the negative reports with Evangeline.

In fact, none of the other supervisors have either; they have only reported their dissatisfaction to Jessica.

Culturally Ineffective: Dysfunctional Rescuing: the Help That Doesn't Help

Jessica, in the most well-meaning way possible, is setting up Evangeline for failure. My colleague Valerie Batts of Visions, Inc., has labeled this "dysfunctional rescuing," a form of "modern oppression." I call it "sloppy sentimentalism," a term borrowed from the renowned black educator, Kenneth Clark. It's the way people in the one-up group treat those from the one-down group because they think the one-down group isn't capable of performing at the required standard. In Jessica's case, she may not be conscious that she is acting from a worry that Evangeline, while talented, isn't talented enough. Try on this idea: sometimes when we think we are helping individuals from one-down groups by providing them opportunities and mentoring, we may still be expecting them to fail. Upsetting, I know, but it happens mostly without our recognition.

Sloppy sentimentalism happens when a manager finds it hard to give negative feedback to a supervisee from a one-down group or to hold the supervisee accountable for his or her behavior. Out of a sense of superiority, someone from a one-up group may decide what is best for someone from a one-down group without asking what the person needs or wants. It's sloppy sentimentalism when, for example, a man at work decides on his own that a woman with children shouldn't be on a project that involves travel or shouldn't be on a project involving a difficult, demanding, or disrespectful client. It's also sloppy sentimentalism when a supervisee might be given less challenging work assignments or responsibilities even when there is no evidence that he or she isn't capable of doing higher-level work. When we have internalized someone's one-down status, we might avoid holding them accountable to measurable standards of performance, such as meeting deadlines or completing thorough and accurate work.

In Jessica's case, even though she is committed to diversity and wants to see all groups of people succeed in the institution, she, like many people from a one-up group, may worry that she will say the wrong thing and be perceived as biased if she is critical. She may believe she is reserving judgment—when, in effect, it is her decision not to offer constructive feedback in this case that reveals her bias.

When you believe in people's abilities and they make mistakes, you correct them and expect them to be able to use that critique to improve. The impact of Jessica's culturally ineffective behavior on Evangeline is certain failure. After which, Jessica, the training-program planners, and the company will engage in considerable hand-wringing and soul-searching. When critical feedback and growth opportunities are withheld, a supervisee is put at a disadvantage. If Evangeline is not told what her shortcomings are, she will not develop sufficiently and will have no idea that she is underperforming until it is too late. Evangeline will be blindsided by the final decision not to hire her and wonder if a program to support diversity had actually treated her unfairly because of her diversity. Sometimes in this situation, the company, being eager to increase its diversity, will nevertheless hire Evangeline, and she will be promoted to a permanent position without being told about her challenges. Instead she will carry these issues into the job until she is undone by them.

Tips for Practicing This Culturally Effective Habit: Keep Your Standards High

- Expect success. Most people perform up to expectations, if you communicate that you have high expectations *and* that you expect them to be met. When

105

you show this kind of confidence in an individual and concern for his or her career development, any critical feedback you have to offer will be more easily accepted and put in its proper context.

- Give good accounts and challenging assignments first; then if the person doesn't do well, consider less demanding or more developmental work—make sure you are not testing a person but are assuming success and supporting that success from the beginning.

- If you are a mentor and hear critical feedback about your protégé, do some investigating first to get a clear understanding of the problem and to determine whether you think the critique is fair; discuss it with your mentee and offer the resources he or she needs to shore up any weaknesses. Even if the critique is unfair, your protégé needs to know the story people are telling so that, with your help, he or she can navigate around, refute, or minimize the damage or concerns.

- If you recommend people to be hired or promoted, make sure that you are looking objectively at their chances for success in your environment. Don't be overly critical or demand that the people from the one-down group be more qualified that their peers from the one-up group. In other words, don't get caught up in what I call the "prince syndrome," looking for an amazing candidate who far exceeds everyone else. But also, don't be undercritical. If you see potential and believe that with support the person can develop the competencies required for the job, that is fine, but you have to make sure both the potential and support are there first.

- Don't ignore problems early on; it is harder to correct issues later, and if the person gets too far behind, it will be harder to catch up. Make your standards and expectations clear and don't expect that they are obvious to everyone.

- If you avoid sloppy sentimentalism, you can still offer support and encourage questions—sometimes people from one-down groups worry that they will be perceived as stupid or inadequate if they ask questions. Many people don't have a quick start when they come into a new environment, especially those who are the "firsts" in their families. They need clear guidance, expectations, support and correction.
- If you think your mentees or supervisees are ultimately not going to be able to succeed because either they lack the competencies to perform at the level required or it will take them too long to gain the necessary capabilities, then help them to make plans for the best next step to continue their careers within or outside your organization.

HABIT #23: AVOID THE ONE-MISTAKE RULE
APPLY CRITERIA FAIRLY

Jackson was recently hired as an intern at a public relations firm. He was excited to learn more about this field, which he intended to make his major in college. Jackson did not go directly to college after high school; he had been in the first Iraq war, and then suffered from severe depression for approximately eighteen months following his discharge. He was now ready to get his degree and start working toward a successful career. Because of his age and experience (he was twenty-seven at the time), he was particularly excited by the prospect of getting outside the classroom and having real-world experiences that could educate him in a way different from textbooks and lectures. His work at the firm was universally praised, and as the weeks went on, Jackson even began to dream about having a job there after he graduated. Then a situation occurred in which he misunderstood what his supervisor wanted him to do; the mistake resulted in a temporary rupture between a client and the firm, which was patched up soon thereafter. Nonetheless, Jackson was told that his services were no longer needed—the firm would sign his internship papers, but he was not to report to work any longer. His supervisor made the offhand comments that he had thought all along that "Jackson would have trouble fitting in" and "you can't teach an old dog new tricks."

Culturally Ineffective: No Room for Error

Often one-down groups have the experience of seeing their mistakes magnified and their accomplishments minimized. In this case, Jackson came from a few different one-down or underrepresented groups: he was older than most interns; he was a veteran and he had suffered from some mental health issues (although this was unknown to his employer at the time). Frequently, individuals from one-down or underrepresented groups have to overcome the stereotype that they are not as bright or as capable as others. When the individuals fail to deliver as expected on one project, misspell one word, miss a single deadline, or analyze a solitary issue incorrectly, the presumption is that that they aren't ready, aren't right for or intelligent enough to do the job properly.

I call this the "one-mistake rule." Jackson upset his supervisor, but this alone does not mean that he is incompetent, irresponsible, or has bad judgment especially in light of his prior positive assessments. It is very possible that his supervisor fell into the one-mistake trap without thinking about it. Subconsciously, however, his supervisor may have been holding an assumption of Jackson's inadequacies, of which his one mistake was the proof. With these attitudes, it would be hard for the supervisor to apply the relevant criteria to Jackson's performance fairly. We know this because of the thinly veiled reference to Jackson's fit and age. Jackson's supervisor may have had a previous negative experience hiring a person who was joining or re-joining the workforce later in life, and who did not perform well, so he now has the expectation that every such intern will have performance issues. I call this type of bias "guilt by association." The supervisor might also be operating on stereotypes against veterans. Although many people cheer and support veterans when they are in the military or when they arrive home, studies suggest that veterans suffer bias when they attempt to reenter the job market. Some employers worry about PTSD and how well those who served can successfully integrate into a corporate work culture.

For Jackson, the problem with this type of cultural ineffectiveness is obvious. His opportunity to prove his abilities and thus the prospect for realizing his dreams in this institution have been abruptly interrupted. His "failure" in this position may have negative implications for his next position if he can't obtain the experience or the enthusiastic references from the firm that make internships worthwhile. He also might begin to doubt himself. But the less apparent cost of this kind of bias is that the company is missing out on what Jackson could have contributed and it may suffer a negative reputation if he tells others about his experience, thereby making it harder for the firm to attract other talented interns from the armed forces.

For Jackson's boss, the problem with this type of cultural ineffectiveness is less obvious. Yet the fact remains that if Jackson's performance record had been mistake-free until now, then perhaps he had not been properly trained to perform well in this situation. By relying on the one-mistake rule, Jackson's boss found a convenient way to avoid looking at himself or his own responsibility for what went wrong.

Tips for Practicing This Culturally Effective Habit :
Apply Criteria Fairly

- In situations where the person you are supervising is a member of a one-down or underrepresented group, or came into the organization in a less traditional path, you need to investigate your assessments so that they are neither made too quickly, nor on the basis of automatic associations that may be influenced by negative stereotypes.
- To apply criteria fairly, you have to make sure you know what the criteria are for the job or task. Also consider whether these requirements have been made clear to the individual you are supervising. So many times, what it takes to be successful in an organization or on a project is not articulated. Success is based on unwritten rules and the ability to navigate underlying cultural norms. Without someone to decode these rules and norms, newcomers, those

111

from one-down groups, and those from non-traditional backgrounds, find it difficult to perform in accordance with their capabilities.

- Ask yourself, "If this person were… (add the relevant one-up group status: straight, white, without a disability, male, Protestant, etc.), how would I assess this situation?" In Jackson's story, his supervisor might ask himself, "Have I had a similar circumstance with a younger intern who followed a more traditional path? How did I evaluate him or her?" Studies on cognitive bias describe something called "leniency bias"—we apply criteria flexibly with those like ourselves (the in-group) and more strictly to those in the out-group.

- Look at the entirety of the person's performance. Considering the person's experience level—do you have enough information about his or her work? Are you being too hasty?

- Consider your work experience. What mistakes did you make? How were your mistakes regarded? Were those assessments fair?

- Evaluate how you and others might have affected the person's performance. Were you clear with your direction and expectations? Did you make assumptions about what the supervisee knew? Were you direct? You may be attributing the problem solely to that person (or some aspect of their identity and background) when there are other contributing factors, including the work and responsibility of other individuals.

- Encourage questions. As mentioned earlier, sometimes individuals from one-down groups know the stereotype that haunts them. They often do not ask questions about assignments because they don't want to run the risk of saying something that may confirm any negative perception in their supervisor's mind. Of course, in many instances, this concern prevents them from getting the information they need to perform successfully. Make sure you encourage questions and offer information and other resources that will support that person's success.

- Finally, don't be afraid, as we explained in Habit #22, "Don't be a Sloppy Sentimentalist," to have a conversation with the person to share your interpretation of events that have occurred. Your honest appraisal of the situation will likely be of great use for your supervisee if you offer it in a constructive spirit and welcome the supervisee's understanding of what went wrong.

- To learn more about how to hire and support veterans who are re-entering the workforce visit Career One Stop, www.careeronestop.org, or the U.S. Department of Veteran Affairs www.vesuccess.gov.

113

HABIT #24: AHAS MAKE THE DIFFERENCE
GET SOME GOOD DIVERSITY TRAINING

When I first got started in diversity work, I was the head of an organization whose mission was to attract more talented people of color to the Boston legal community. As such, I sponsored a number of informative events about diversity and various dialogues about the problems confronting attorneys of color, the profession, and the city. We also had short diversity trainings that allowed us to learn about basic diversity concepts. However, one day, because I was considering becoming a trainer myself, I attended a two-day, anti-bias training, and my world changed. First, it was great to be surrounded by people from different backgrounds and occupations who had elected to, as we say in the business, "do the work"—wrestling with deep concepts of culture, prejudice, privilege, oppression, and exclusion in themselves and society.

There was one exercise from that workshop that I still remember because it made me cry for days. One by one, individuals volunteered to stand in front of the group and describe a time they were mistreated because of a difference. The stories that people told were so moving—both crushing and inspiring at the same time. I remember one person who spoke about how she stopped talking for years when she was a little kid because of how she was teased about her accent. Others shared indignities suffered in the workplace that were ignored and, as a result, caused them to abandon their dreams. On the other hand, some incidents ended in victories won through determination and stamina, despite opportunities unfairly denied. After they shared their stories, the volunteers were encouraged to speak out about what they wished someone had done differently to prevent or interrupt the mistreatment they suffered. Then we, as the listeners, were asked to put up our hands and promise to remember the story, and then to make an increased commitment to stand up against the particular *ism* (racism, sexism, elitism, ageism, etc.) they had endured. The exercise changed me forever and deepened my commitment to make a difference in my life and the lives of others.

Culturally Ineffective: "Can You Do a Training in Two Hours? And Please, None of That Touchy-Feely Stuff"

When did *touching* and *feeling* become such bad words? So many highly educated people tell me that they care about diversity and inclusion and want to learn more, but in the same breath they say, "But you're not going to get all touchy-feely with us, right?'" It is hard to be culturally effective without feeling. So much about getting good at this work has nothing to do with cognitive intelligence. In fact, real progress usually begins when we develop emotional, social, and spiritual intelligence—when we humble ourselves to learn what we don't know. Since that first workshop I attended, I have participated in many others, sometimes for four days at a stretch. I have seen how important engaging the intellect is, but far more powerful are experiences where people go beyond what they already know, get out of their comfort zones, and learn to empathize. This is how I like to shape my own workshops, sharing cognitive and data-driven information, but also providing ample opportunity for discussion and exercises that cause people to feel something or come upon a realization they hadn't had before. People call it having an "aha moment" when awareness breaks through or paradigms shift. These kinds of group experiences help you to explore your culture, your one-up and one-down identities, and the direct impact of stereotypes, power and privilege. They also increase your awareness of the struggles and strengths of other groups.

There are so many types of trainings that you can participate in to "do the work" of getting a better understanding of how identity and culture shape all of our experiences. This is work that you can't do by yourself—by only reading a book or being a good person. You have to be with other people, sharing their journeys and examining your own; without these types of conversations, you may never have access to such information and you will always be worried about saying the wrong thing. It can also be highly beneficial to do this work with professionals who can lead you through a framework of exercises so that you can learn the specific ways you can move diversity forward. Having a certain period of time set aside to learn advanced set of tools often speeds up the process and focuses everyone involved.

Tips for Practicing This Culturally Effective Habit: Get Some Good Diversity Training

- Avail yourself of training opportunities wherever they may be found: at your children's school, your place of worship, your job, and so on. You can also look into attending anti bias (racism, sexism, etc.) trainings offered by various groups such as the YWCA, Visions, Inc., and National Coalition Building Institute. These trainings will give you a chance to interact with people you may not know or allow you to know other people better because you are exploring the context of their cultural identities and experiences. When trainings are done correctly, they create more understanding and cohesion within groups.
- Participate in intragroup workshops, where you spend time talking with your own group about cultural issues. These workshops give you the safety and freedom to share your most difficult concerns and challenges. They also allow you to learn from others in your group about how to be more culturally effective rather than relying on people from the other culture to provide that information for you. If you are white, consider attending the White Privilege

Conference, an amazing event. Thousands of people attend each year and say it is a life-changing experience.

- Approach any training, whether chosen or strongly recommended, with an open and self-reflective mind. Be prepared to listen to the views of others and be willing to share your own views and perspectives. Use a no-shame-blame-or-attack approach. None of us know all that we wished we knew. There are real reasons we aren't as culturally effective as we want to be. Blaming and shaming ourselves or others does not advance the conversation or learning, so endeavor not to feel guilty or to shame others as you interact in the workshop. Ask questions; it's your opportunity to say the wrong thing in a safe environment.

- Realize that training is not a fix-all. Pre- and post-training work make trainings most useful. For successful workplace trainings, the organization needs to be ready to take advantage of the workshops, which means that the workshops are taking place within a larger diversity initiative—the leaders are on board and committed to change, and the value of diversity has been identified and linked to the organization's mission. Time should be spent prior to the training assessing the particular issues at play in the environment and making sure the trainer knows about them. Most trainers will ask to interview people so that they can shape the content of the workshop to make it relevant and effective. And after the training there should be follow-up and ways to keep the conversation going as well as continual evaluation and revision of practices, systems, and policies to support increased diversity and inclusion.

- Leaders should be trained first. Many times organizations start training those at the bottom of the organizational chart because they perceive less resistance to the idea or because this group can be required to participate. Interestingly enough, this part of the organization is often the most diverse and is usually better versed at these issues. If the owners and decision makers are too busy for this very important work, it's a sign that true commitment is lacking. It means they don't fully understand cultural effectiveness, which is about the institution having the best talent functioning at the highest potential and helping to bring the diverse perspectives and networks that the organization needs to be strong and relevant into the future. When leaders aren't aware and equipped to be culturally effective, they can sabotage all the work of diversity in the institution by making decisions and policies and taking actions that impede inclusion.

- Keep the trainings happening. Training is not a one-time thing. The more you endeavor to be culturally effective, the more you will see the onion: layers and layers of a multidimensional set of issues and understandings. You will not be diversified with one training! Also, organizations may decide to do additional and separate trainings for leaders, newcomers, managers, leaders' supervisors, women, people of color, LGBT individuals, hiring personnel, and so forth. Different groups have different responsibilities and experiences within the organization and often benefit from trainings specific to those roles and differences.

- Finally, don't wait for your organizations to conduct trainings. It is important to do this work with others, as we mentioned, but it is also necessary that you undertake to educate yourself. You can read books, watch television programs, or go to see films that feature the various experiences, culture, and history of groups of people to whom you have had little or no exposure. You may be surprised to find that the work of increasing your exposure is a *both-and* experience: you will both notice the human commonalities we all share,

119

and you will see how our seemingly shared educational, legal, political, and media systems affect us differently depending on our one-down or one-up status. Whichever route you choose, the important thing is to learn what it feels like to walk a mile in another's shoes. Experiencing a fertile cross-section of different perspectives will both expand your worldview and develop your confidence when it comes to navigating diversity issues.

HABIT #25: TAKE THE CHALLENGE
BE RESPONSIBLE FOR ANOTHER'S SUCCESS

When I was the executive director of a diversity organization in Boston, the Attorney General of Massachusetts at the time, Scott Harshbarger, a white, middle-aged man, saw me make a presentation and called to say, "You're really good. You should work for me. I want my office to be more diverse, and I want it to better serve the diverse citizens of our state. Can you help me do that?" After some discussion, I decided to take him up on the offer, first as a consultant and then as his Deputy Chief of Staff. Throughout the time I worked for the office, I was aware of many of the ways he invested in my career. He named me Deputy Chief and gave me a direct reporting structure with other top management, which signified the importance of diversity and it gave me access to him as a leader. While Scott demanded accountability, he gave me great leeway to create policies and practices to enhance more diversity and inclusion. As the leader, he vocally and visibly supported these policies and made it clear why they made the office better. Whenever I wavered about taking a certain position on a diversity-related issue with other leaders or agencies, I would tell him, "I don't know if I can ask that of the Division Chiefs." And he would respond, "You know what you are talking about; you don't need me, but if you have trouble, let me know." He invited me to be at the table with internal and external leaders for discussions of policies and decisions—some of which weren't directly related to diversity and outreach. That inclusion increased my visibility and gave me opportunities to share my ideas and strengthen my voice. He taught me how to manage and accomplish large projects and demonstrated confidence in me even when I made mistakes. During this time, we made great strides in diversity in the office and with our constituents. After working with the Attorney General, I went onto start my own consulting firm.

Culturally Ineffective: "I Took My Mentee to Lunch; Now I'm All Set"

In every organization, there are leaders who have the power, influence, and gravitas that they could use to ensure the success of talented people from a one-down group in their organization. If every one of them had this as a goal, we would see diversity moving forward much more quickly. This is the idea of sponsorship, which goes beyond mentoring someone. Mentoring can happen in a moment, over a month, or during a particular project. To be culturally effective as a sponsor, however—to be responsible for another's success—means doing more than giving advice on substantive work and cultural norms. It extends beyond countering biases like sloppy sentimentalism and the one-mistake rule—it means reversing their impact. Very exciting!

The Attorney General was very instrumental in reversing the impact that negative bias and my cultural conditioning as a woman of color from a working-class family had had in my own life. One of the ways he did this was to make me aware of how I was undercutting my own power. After making a presentation one day, I asked the Attorney General for feedback. Without missing a beat he said, "You were great, once you stopped apologizing for the lights and the temperature of the room." I was shocked and protested, "I don't do that!" Scott explained that not only did I do it that morning, but every time I spoke I started off with an apology, usually for something over which I had no control. After some reflection, I realized that my cultural programming as a person of color and my socialization as a woman shaped how I made presentations; while there may have been nothing inherently wrong with this way of being, as a leader in that environment, it rendered me less effective than I could otherwise have been. From then on, whenever I stood before and audience, I would feel the apology bubbling up inside of me, but then I would replace it with a bold beginning statement. The Attorney General was right; I felt more powerful as a result.

Sponsoring others and feeling invested in their ultimate success happens every day in our institutions; it just happens less frequently for people from one-down groups. Because many in positions of power are from one-up groups in race, ethnicity, gender, and sexual orientation, sponsoring others in one-up groups flows more naturally for them because of their instinctive identification and comfort with these individuals. But if we are going to be culturally effective, we must consciously go looking for the opportunity to ensure the success of those who are not like us. If you are in a position of responsibility, this is the perfect time to go all out. If you are in a position of relative power, use your gravitas to identify and provide challenging and career-defining assignments and opportunities for someone from a one-down group, ensuring that that person is recognized for his or her contributions and is fairly compensated. Sponsoring or championing someone to ensure advancement is far from impossible once we decide to be intentional about it. In the end, you will view the success of such an undertaking as one of the capstones of your career.

123

Tips for Practicing This Culturally Effective Habit: Be Responsible for Another's Success

- First, notice that you have the power to make a difference and decide that you will use that power. This is a big move, but I say, "If you've got it, flaunt it!" You probably have already made this move for others in a one-up group, so you may already know what to do—you just have to decide consciously to select someone from the one-down group to benefit this time. You are electing to be what people refer to as a sponsor or champion.
- Start looking around. Who in your world, in your sphere of influence, could

you take on to make a difference in their life and career pursuits? You are looking for someone who has potential and needs a godfather or godmother to translate all that hard work and ability into success at the highest levels. It could be someone for whom English is a second language; it could be a person in your division with a disability. It might be a Muslim American mother on your board. It could be a passionate and hard-working black woman like me from a humble background, someone who was a little rough around the edges and overly apologetic, but who could shine and elevate your mission for the organization with the right guidance and opportunity.

- Think about who your "rabbis" were. What did they do to help you get where you are? What did they overlook or have to correct? To what lengths were they willing to go to introduce you to the right people or help you to navigate away from the wrong people? Don't be stingy with your resources and connections. You can make introductions to others inside and outside the organization who can help create opportunities.

- Help the person strategize and map out a plan for his or her career. Some people are doing great in their present positions, but they have their heads down working so hard and trying to prove themselves that they don't have a plan for the future. When an opportunity comes to advance, then they are not well positioned to take advantage of it, or they find themselves in the wrong department or on the wrong project. Having someone who has been there and done well with whom they can do some forecasting can be very powerful.

- Provide advice about how to address misperceptions, disappointments, and biases that may be negatively affecting your sponsee's standing. When a person knows you are invested in her success, you can have honest conversations with them about what needs to change in order for her to continue to progress. It's very hard for sponsees to see themselves, especially when they are trying to succeed in an environment that may not be representative of or receptive to who they are.

- Intervene on someone's behalf when you feel standing up for the person is justified and necessary, especially when it comes to assignments, promotions, and compensation. Often these are critical junctures where biases put those in the one-down group at a disadvantage. People from the one-down group often are asked to wait or prove again and again that their good performance in not a fluke. Because of leniency bias, which we mentioned earlier, for those in the one-up group criteria for opportunity are applied more flexibly. In other words, even when those in the one-up group may not have satisfied all the requirement, they are judged on their potential and the assumption that they will get there—bias runs in their favor. Women, women with children, people of color, immigrants, and other one-down group members, however, are judged more strictly on what they have achieved at the time of the evaluation, and even that may be discounted by the descriptive bias as mentioned in Habit #13, "Are You Sure You're A Doctor." They just don't look like the description people have in their heads about who belongs in the position.

- Be prepared to vouch for and promote your person. It doesn't matter that you mentor and strategize with a person if you are not willing to say to those who matter, "This person is exactly the person you want!" It is important to let people know what the person has accomplished and even be willing to get righteously angry on the person's behalf. Often when one-down people stand up for themselves, share their accomplishments, or act passsionately or forthrightly, their behavior is not interpreted the same way it would be if they were from a one-up group. Women who self-promote and stand up for themselves, for example, are sometimes seen as not team players, or out for themselves, or too aggressive. Your stamp of approval as a one-up person goes a long way to alleviate these issues. Helping others to see the talent and possibilities that you see in the person accelerates the forward movement of diversity.

- Get familiar with the idea that bias exists in you and in the world in which the person you are championing is trying to succeed. Be the type of champion who is open to learning and hearing about these issues. The Attorney General had such a wonderful combination of self-awareness and personal confidence that he asked me to guide and tutor him on racial and other diversity issues. I knew he was a serious student when one day he called me after attending a parade in Massachusetts and said, "Something didn't feel right at the parade today; there were no people of color. Where were they? We need to fix this!"

INDEX